RACE REGENERATION
The Mystery of Sex

A Course of Instruction on the Right
Use of Sex.

BY R. SWINBURNE CLYMER, M. D

Graduate College of Medicine and
Surgery, Chicago, 1902.

Author of "Diet, The Way to Health",
"Making Health Certain", "Higher
Race Development", etc., etc.

♂

Published by

The Humanitarian Society
"Beverly Hall,"
Quakertown, Pa.

Kessinger Publishing's Rare Reprints
Thousands of Scarce and Hard-to-Find Books!

Introductory

First Edition

This volume goes forth without apology.

Excuses are necessary only under two conditions: In case of mistakes, or where one foists upon the public something uncalled for; neither of these apply to the author of this book.

The instructions found herein have been tested. After an experience of eighteen years we pronounce them sound and practical. The members and workers of the Rose Cross Aid,* in their many sessions, have added their approval and commendation. This society, taking a leading part in Reconstruction work, requested that these lessons be issued in book form; through the generosity of Rev. A. W. Witt, and several others, this has been made financially possible.

From an unlimited experience in dealing with thousands of men and women sexually weak or disabled, we are in a position to state positively that sex truths should be taught to every human being. A knowledge of the use (and abuse) of the creative nature is as imperative to right living, as a chaste life is essential to health. Neither is possible when the sex function is abused; our varied experience teaching us that most of the ailments classed as "neurotic" can frequently be traced directly to sexual abnormality and premature weakness. *This remedied, health results.*

We select two reasons, out of many, for the publication of this book, and outline them briefly:

First: The increasing prevalency of the insidious argument in favor of continence. We feel a positive duty in refuting

---

*The Rose Cross Aid has merged with the Humanitarian Society, since the publication of the first edition of this book.

this monstrous doctrine. To illustrate a single point in this matter we quote from a noted writer and advocate of this undesirable practice: "It is scarcely necessary to say that all testimony concurs in forbidding indulgence during gestation * * * * * The fact that fecundation would be impossible during pregnancy, and that during this period the female, normally, has no sexual desire, are other powerful arguments in favor of perfect continence at this time."

This superficial argument, accepted by many as truth, is far from it. Such statements will not bear careful investigation. In our varied and extensive practice and experience in sex psychology and psycha-analysis, we have been able to obtain facts "first hand" and ninety per cent. of the women questioned admitted that sexual embrace was actually a necessity during pregnancy that in the instances where the husbands failed to agree with them they often passed sleepless nights. This sex hunger undoubtedly makes a deep impression upon the unborn child and we maintain that many of the abnormal conditions found in children are the result of such denial.

We would *not* for a moment advocate sexual embrace in all cases during the period of pregnancy. It depends entirely upon the nature of the individual woman. But we do state emphatically that a normal condition should be treated so; that is, the natural desire should be satisfied. When the love nature of a pregnant woman is aroused sexual communion should be indulged in without hesitation. A woman is none the less a wife because motherhood confronts her.

We are at variance with the whole idea of the so-called sublimity of the continent life. Nothing could be more absurd. Our basic claim is that a woman who has lived a continent life cannot have fulfilled the best and highest in her; that unknown and unawakened powers dwell therein, hence she is guilty of "hiding these talents" instead of making use of them and risking their loss, as biblical authority advocates for *all* of man's powers, forces, and possessions.

Once in a while we find a woman who has loved sincerely and deeply and been deprived of the object of that love through no fault of her own. The shock of the loss deadened the love nature completely, and to her the sexual embrace would be loathsome, in fact, a prostitution. Such a woman can turn her energy into another line of creation—that of work, for example, and live a successful life. But a case like this is an exception to prove the rule; not one woman in fifty thousand has a deadened love nature from such a cause.

The second reason for the publication of this book: The necessity of sex instruction to every human being. A personal experience may illustrate the point.

On Thursday, August 9, 1917, a woman in this vicinity was taken in travail and a physician summoned. The child was born before he arrived. No provision whatever had been made for the care of the mother or the reception of the baby. Not a stitch of clothing had been prepared, not even a band.

The doctor found the woman lying on an old mattress of straw, some of which had fallen through the rents to the uncarpeted floor. Not only the bed and covering, but the entire room was in a state of filthiness difficult to describe.

Assuming charge of this unhappy, disgusting situation, the physician asked for a towel. Not one could be found, and on being proffered a dirty piece of cloth, he was forced to abandon precaution and take care of the patient with unwashed hands rather than risk infection from the use of the rags.

The confinement taking place in the evening there was only one thing to do—wrap up the child in some old clothing and allow it to remain in that condition until morning.

The physician having to devote the next day to examination of conscripts, we were requested to take charge of the case. We found the woman, normal and seemingly happy, and the child just as it had been left the night before. In the day light the filth was even more frightful, vermin crawling over the newborn baby.

But the worst feature of the picture is still to be presented. Sitting on the bed was another child, a little girl perhaps two years old who, without any interference from the mother, *was practicing self-abuse.*

Can one imagine anything more terrible? What chance has a child born under a roof like that? What can be expected of the children born of ignorant, degraded parents like these? How can any man or woman say that sex instruction is unnecessary? Is it not a God-given task to better the conditions under which so many babies are born? Let the thinking man and woman answer. This is only one case out of a *multitude of similar ones.*

R. Swinburne Clymer.

"Beverly Hall"
Quakertown, Pa.
Oct. 20, 1918.

Foreword to Second Edition

Two reasons were offered for the publication of the first edition of this book; these need no repetition here; they again appear in the "Introductory remarks."

The motive for the reissue of the work in a revised and much enlarged form is in no wise changed, though two other considerations have had much influence in hastening the publication of a rewritten edition, namely:

First: The reception given the book. The entire edition selling within a short time, while not a single comment adverse to its contents, has ever been received.

Second: The rapidity with which the practice of homosexuality, auto- and mutual erotism, and the teachings of birth-control advocates are spreading among the white race, leading to decadence and self-deterioration; and, if allowed to continue, the ultimate destruction of these peoples.

Referring to the Chapters such as "Babylonianism," "Conjugal Fraud," "Spiritual Significance of Sex" Part two, and "Birth Control," we request the reader to carefully note all quotation marks so as not to inadvertently place upon us the odius of being guilty of promulgating the reprehensible and destructive teachings within them.

In these several chapters we have extensively quoted from several widely read authors; deeming it far better to quote *verbatim* than to offer our personal conceptions of what we might think they taught, because in several instances the themes are so vile that we do not care to be held responsible for a misunderstanding. *All such quotations appear with quotation marks;* while our comments, whether comprising but a few words, or several paragraphs, without any marks whatever.

Throughout the book, we have interspersed, under the caption of "The Great Madness" news items as they appeared in the various newspapers of the country. These reports are in most instances *verbatim* and in quotation marks; our comments on the items appearing without any marks whatever.

We have used the title: "The Great Madness" because the acts of men and women portrayed in them are rapidly leading the people, especially the unthinking classes (the masses), to a state of chaos; a mental concept of life having respect for neither law, order, religion or authority; such a situation is certain to bring the nation to the brink of ruin, if not to actual destruction, unless men of strength, guided by wisdom, take the helm of the ship of state.

The Humanitarian Society has thus far issued more than a million leaflets and booklets; has reached possibly six million of people with its various publications, and counts fifty thousand adherents to its work. All of the publications inculcating obedience to just legislation, or the orderly repeal of class statutes affecting the many while exempting the few; a belief in the Fatherhood of God and necessity for religion, and a full freedom permitting every one affiliation with the denomination of choice, without consideration as to its strength or weakness; respect for state and parental authority; the open platform for science, with the privilege of accepting or refusing conclusions reached; the natural life; the sacredness of sex, and its potency for reconstruction or destruction.

We are perfectly willing to allow the reader to form his own judgment of the value of the book here offered and will appreciate criticism from those who have the welfare of the race at heart.

R. Swinburne Clymer.

"Beverly Hall"
Quakertown, Pa.
Jan. 7th, 1921.

The Purity of Sex

To the Pure in Heart All Things Are Pure

The same general proverbs, adages, and axioms, are found among all peoples; irrespective of the age, source, or to whom especially addressed, there is a similarity in the enunciation of moral truths. "Unto the pure all things are pure," has found its way through many holy books of the long past, as well as in the Bible of our own time. Men agree with this quotation without hesitation until the subject of sex is introduced, then retire in confusion—inner guilt benumbs the senses.

In the vegetable and animal kingdoms the law governing mating and reproduction, is accepted as a matter of course, and men see nothing to be ashamed of in the breeding of animals; selecting the participants, they watch and assist at the birth of the young, feed them and train them, again selecting the future breeders, meanwhile enthusiastically discussing their good and weak points without a thought of either self-consciousness or of concealment. As a matter of fact, many now take great pride in the success attending their efforts in producing superior stock; offence being unthought of, even though plain and bold the language used in discussing the method pursued in breeding. The perpetuation of desirable traits, form and color, and the eradication of questionable qualities are common subjects to thousands upon thousands of breeders of animals, but turn the attention to human reproduction, a subject of *infinitely* greater importance to man and God, and what happens? Every one, almost without exception, will turn aside and seek to cover their ignorance, prejudice, or shame, with a display of supposed righteous virtue.

Dr. J. H. Greer, formerly Professor in the College of Medicine and Surgery, Chicago, lecturing on the subject of sex, said:

"Throughout the domain of nature the instinct of sex is paramount. In the highest kingdom of life the instinct is subject to the modifications of civilization, which, alas, is not always the best. The lives of all men are colored by the thoughts of sex, which may be of the varying shades between good and bad. Asceticism, on the one hand, strives to suppress as impure all thoughts and feelings regarding the relations of the sexes. Those who are so narrow as to conform to the letter while ignoring the spirit of true religion, may be cited as the most baneful of combatants of pure thought on the subject. On the other hand is the unchaste, immoral sensualist, who believes that life means gratification of the senses, the most exquisite of which is the sexual relation. He drains the wine of life to the dregs, and, when at last sated, can see nothing of the true use of the bodily senses. The extremes exist because they do not know the truth."

We would dispel this murky cloud by assisting humanity to a knowledge of the *development of a superior race;* and in the effort avoid both extremes. There is a sane, middle course untinged by any cult or ism, one that we have, through long experience, found worthy of acceptance as a standard of life for all men. This course adjusts sexual and physical inharmonies, bringing in its train health and happiness as the result of *sane exercise* of the Creative functions. Those who have attempted to find truth by following the false path of continence will be benefitted equally with the ones who have pursued the opposite course; that of license and debauchery.

The constructive path lies *midway* between the two extremes and leads to the Fountain of life; aye, to the *Fountain of Youth* so much sought by many. Those that choose this course in life discover the beauty and divinity of sex and quickly recognize the Laws of God controlling the functions, as just and righteous. Correctly understood, the truths concerning sex do not bring a blush to the most saintly cheek; nothing being discoverable in God's laws to humiliate, or mortify, man; the sense of shame belonging *only to those who live life shamefully.*

Why should sex be considered impure? Can it be in itself

degrading? Its abuse may make it so, but of itself it is pure, for *God made all things so;* then why differentiate between humans and animals, giving the latter all that is best in thought and service, as respecting reproduction and the creating of a superior specie, while discouraging and condemning all that concerns the like functions in man? Is not a clean, virtuous, healthy woman God's greatest and most beautiful handiwork, a thousandfold the superior of any animal ever born? Why then is the human feminine degraded by man, and the animal female studied, petted, and developed; their duty and functions being alike in the world of reproduction? The answer is not far to seek: The mind and heart of the males, and many females (not *men* and *women*), have become so perverted, defiled, and unspeakably filthy, from dwelling in lewd thought, upon contact, gratification, and sensations, that the spiritual side has never been recognized by them. The man who can find impurity in sex, who can think of it with any thought but of God's loftiest intention, should undergo a long period of mental, physical, and spiritual cleansing.

One is lost in the labyrinth of futile conjecture when attempting to find an answer for the foulness, ignorance and baseness of many of the male specie. The subject of sex generally bringing a knowing leer to the face, a licentious look to the eye, while unbridled thoughts manifest through the entire organism. Even good and virtuous women, at the mention of the creative function, cast down their eyes, give evasive answers, and hasten a change of discussion from so secret a subject. What has brought humankind to such a mental state of impurity? In the first place, it was undoubtedly a lack of sex instruction and a full understanding of God's Creative function. In the second, the actual encouragement of degraded, perverted, vile, and untruthful ideas. Evil thrives in the darkness of ignorance, and almost every mother in the world, good of heart as she may be, and unquestionably is, has been guilty of instilling in the mind and heart of her children glaring untruth when first they questioned her, *and this is the seed from which all future falsehood, as concerning the reproduction of her kind, springs.* What a fearful indictment of motherhood in an otherwise enlightened age.

It is often maintained that the world is spiritually and morally improving; but trust and faith are required to believe this assertion, when we are confronted with the various forms of license and debauchery rampant in the great cities of today. The history of Sodom and Gomorrha, destroyed by fire because of the unspeakable sex practices of its people, is repeated in this century with a diversity of sex habits that would shame those ancient perverts, who were, in comparison to the moral lepers of the present, mere *dilettante* in sex debasement.

Had a knowledge of sex and its purposes been taught those ancient people, society of today might not be honeycombed with loathesome diseases—*as it is*—nor accursed with the number of degenerates now infesting it. Sex seems always to have been a subject of apology and—*perversion*, given consideration only when the *light was turned out*. Can the wildest fanatic argue that we are better for this past ignoring of a vital subject? Is not the degradation and perversion of sex greatly increased by such a procedure? It is propitious a movement were launched; teaching the creative laws as first instituted by God, to groups and singly, in clubs, schools, and churches, *whether the majority agree or disagree.* Light must be diffused on the darkness of this subject, or the race will die out; and the Humanitarian Society has been instituted with this work as an important part of its program.

If ignorance and secrecy were constructive and desirable, would not the people of the present be far in advance of the ancients, in morality and spirituality,—spirituality being based on purity in sex,—and race improvement? Most assuredly! Regrettably, this is not the fact. Perversion is increasing at an alarming extent, though legal enactments and enforcements have scattered the red light districts and their denizens to the four winds of the earth, thereby greatly diffusing vice. The red light districts, contrary to the general delusion, and at which the world points with scorn, and the subject of self-righteous suppression, are the least harmful in the perpetuation of perversion. The private life, in an uncountable number of homes on the entire face of the earth, reek with defilement and corruption, not alone between men and women, but between men and men, women and women.

Society at large, has little to fear from the inmates of the shadowed districts; through police and medical supervision they can be kept within certain limits. The woman of ill-fame, does not, except in rare instance, *reproduce her kind;* consequently, her influence, compared to that of corrupt homes, is insignificant.

The greatest sex crimes in the human calendar, are perpetuated *in the homes where love is not.* To enjoy, but not to bear children, and in defiance of the Lord's command: "Be fruitful," married couples resort to all manner of degrading practices; and perversion originated in the desire to prevent reproduction, yet not curtail the pleasures of physical satisfaction; *this was the original sin, first committed by Adam and Eve; it was the one apple they were forbidden to eat.*

Vice in the home is doubly destructive; bearing on the public good as well as on the future of the race; and the ultimate result of unnatural practices on the individual themselves are horrible to contemplate. Body, mind, and soul (if there is any) suffer; drugs being resorted to continually, the mind dwelling on debasing practices; the most diabolical of the effects being bequeathed to the children who frequently are born *despite the perversions.* Has the student of methods for race betterment ever asked himself the question, with a mental attitude actually desiring the truth: "Where do all the cripples, idiots, drug fiends, degenerates, and child and woman exploiters, found in the present generation, come from? *We have already offered you the key to the supposed mystery;* though it must *not* be supposed that we maintain the undefendable position that *all* cripples, idiots, and drug fiends, are the result of perversion or sex sins, in the parents.

The enemies of the dissemination of sex knowledge declare

that if instruction, and publicity, is directed toward this subject the result will be far worse than the present position of humanity. Regrettable as this must appear to the humanitarian, the majority of mankind no doubt agree with this verdict, for the majority, it is a notorious fact, are always against mental, physical, and spiritual progression. Why? Because the greater number of human beings are satisfied to allow others to think and plan for them; they look backward to what their fathers thought and did; deeming that condition good enough for themselves, rather than make the effort to help institute an enlightening, advancing, future. It is the few, imbued with the Christic spirit of helpfulness and service, who step forward to lead their plodding and suffering brothers cut of the land of bondage and prejudice, ignorance and bigotry, into a knowledge of God and His laws. An understanding of the problems of sex is no exception; it is just as essential as to possess the knowledge of any other department of life; and when the youths are taught the facts concerning their bodies and their functions as clearly and carefully as students in agricultural colleges are instructed in the breeding and development of the various animals; when sex-health and morality are considered as rational a study as Latin and mathematics, then *vice will no longer be the destructive agency it is at present, because much of the mystery which first attracts the many, will have been dispelled.*

Mystery and curiosity travel hand in hand; secrecy is their sponsor. The small boy, untaught by his father, whispers something obscene to his companion, laughing and gloating over the vileness of the communication, is preparing for future licentious thought and action. Being inquisitive, as all healthy children should be, he seeks to know, and wants to discuss, that which seemingly, because his parents will not enlighten him, is hidden; and in one way or another he will lift the veil; though generally the knowledge he does obtain is not the truth, but an evil interpretation of it; he succumbs to secret vice, and another victim is added to the long list of the great god Ignorance; whereas had his parents fulfilled their sacred trust, had he been given plain facts, and biology taught him in a sane, orderly, reasonable, decent manner, the evil side of the creative force might never have entered his mind.

A very uncouth example illustrates the desirability of openness, frankness, and correct understanding. When women wore very long, clinging skirts, it was no uncommon sight to see men and boys salaciously observing the shapeliness of limbs on a windy day. All were animated by a natural curiosity, wanting to see that which is supposed to be concealed except in the marriage chamber. That particular phase of curiosity is dead, women generally now wear skirts so short that pedal extremities are now so ordinary a sight even husbands are no longer imbued with the natural curiosity so essential to a happy home. That which was once religiously concealed, is now more than revealed; the mystery is disclosed to all who may care to look.

The hideous, noxious, pernicious aspects of sex must be erased from the minds of men, or the race will be foredoomed through a purity turned to foulness. Whole nations *have* been annihilated in the past, as both Biblical and profane history records. The story of the Israelites in the wilderness and the fall of the Roman Empire are ample proof that a people may be quickly wiped from the face of the earth, for the sins of sex debasement.

God made the world and all it contains; He established laws for its welfare and then *pronounced all good*. In the wisdom of the Father certain edicts of sex were included; these He never revoked. Some men would have us believe that He has now turned over an important department of life to be governed by the gross ignorance of men; that after having bestowed one of the greatest of His prerogatives on human kind, He has withdrawn Himself, thereby acquiesing to the chaos that has resulted. The power to create, the privilege of generation and *regeneration* through right use of sex was not a whim or an accident of the great Creative God, but an eternal law given to men for a definite purpose, as fixed and unchangeable as that which governs the stars in their courses. Woe to that man, society, or nation, who attempts to subvert a law of the great Father of all.

The nations of the earth now undermined with venereal diseases can be enlightened and saved through the education and direction of the individuals composing it. Reverence, and purity of desire are the first two requisites; and undoubtedly these qualities were in the thought of Jesus when he said: "Unless ye become as little children ye can in no wise enter the kingdom of heaven."

Men must return to, or acquire, the attitude of the child; the purity of mind and heart without which the laws and reasons of sex cannot be correctly understood. It is unquestionably a far stretch of the imagination to rehabilitate the base, vulgar mind of a degenerate man; thinking it possible for him to return to the state of God-like purity possessed by the child-mind, but *unless he does*, he must remain a wreck and an outcast, and no power in earth or heaven, no faith or creed, can reach or save him. Thousands upon thousands of these derelicts will continue in the path of destruction; and with an "unconscious" feeling of loathing, mingled with pity, perhaps, we pass them by; *but the younger generation must be taught and rescued from this awful fate.* The children, still pure in thought, must be kept so; while those whose thoughts and acts are now tainted with misuse and unholy desires must be turned quickly and the evil replaced with good; while the young men and women must be appealed to, must be familiarized with the consequences of ignorance, and in the name of all that is Holy and Sacred, taught the exalted use of the reproductive functions of their being. The older generation, the fathers and mothers of the present, must be forced, through continuous inculcation of these truths, to recognize their responsibility, not alone in the preservation of their own minds and bodies, but likewise in the guidance of their offspring.

It must be thoroughly drilled in the minds of the young, middle aged, and the old, that the entire sex function was organized by God and therefore cannot in itself be either unclean or impure. The use of the organism is just as normal as that of the stomach or any other part of the body. God did not create the function to be shunned or slighted; nor to be the basis, the laboratory, for obscene thoughts and actions; neither something to be ashamed of and degraded when darkness covers the earth; thus being catalogued as evil along with other destructive agencies that work in the night.

Is it not an uplifting, ennobling thought for men, made in the image of the Father, to believe that He created them in such form, and with potencies, for which they must forever be apologizing? Yet this is just what the majority of "he" and "she" creatures are continuously doing.

Sex is pure; it is holy and exalting; and employed in the love-embrace its *potency is beyond compute*. In the correct use of sex, in generation and regeneration, man is endowed with a power angels might envy.(*) Instead of striving to understand the laws governing this great privilege and possession of power, man continuously tramples this greatest gift of a just God in the mire of sensuality and ignorance; thus failing ever to realize the *holiness of the function,* the halo of glory that should attend its employment; wallowing in perversions and voluntarily seeking the way to physical, moral, and spiritual ruin.

The abuse of the creative function is the sole cause for the general thought of impurity concerning it. Good and pure in itself, it has been violated by the "demons of sense gratification," until the thoughts of men are distorted and they see falsity as truth. Men, having defiled a benefaction of God, turn the use of a pure function into unholy channels and then declare sex manifestations unclean and unfit for those spiritually inclined.

It is utterly impossible for a healthy, normal, noble-minded man (we include the spiritual eunuchs of present-day organizations), who has employed his creative forces as the Creator intended he should, to think of sex with lewdness, or to consider it unholy or impure. To such an enlightened man (or woman),

---

*The "Arcanum of Sex" is a series of private instructions on this important subject, prepared for those few who are seeking for the exact truth; desiring to know the potential force and energy to be obtained through exalting the Creative powers.

one part of his body is neither better, nor worse, than another. For "unto the pure *all* things are pure," said the master-teacher.

The development of a *superior race* must be brought about through the education of men in the correct use of the creative function; the fundamental laws must be freely taught, without bias, fear, or favor.

God created all things in purity; when children are answered truthfully as soon as they commence to ask questions, and taught to give the creative organism the respect due it; when they are apprised of the powers, purposes, and requirements of the sex nature; when they are so instructed that every detail is understood, morbid, unhealthy thought and desire will vanish, mystery disappear, and the shameful, destructive practices and perversions fade as dreams of the past.

The Beginning of Sex Lies

A noted prelate of one of the largest and most powerful religious organizations of the western world is said to have made the remark that, if his church could but control the first nine years of a child's life, it mattered little what after-influences might be brought to bear, the teachings inculcated could never be eradicated from the child's mind or heart.

Generally this is true; the first impressions on the plastic mind of the child are indelible; but why confine the child's true education to the doctrines of the parent's particular church or creed? Is it not more important to teach the youth the *mysteries of being* as it is to drill into their minds the history of the saints; the necessity of observing special days in the church calendar or the preparation for an existence beyond the grave? Children are consistently taught the basic elements of a faith for the preservation of their souls *after* death; but the fundamentals of **biology and sexology**, having as their object the preservation of physical life, which is the basis, not only of health, happiness and evolution, but the *welfare of the soul itself*, are almost entirely ignored and left to chance. *The immortalization of the soul is definitely related to the regeneration of the body.* It is just as imperative to know and obey God's laws governing the physical world as it is to follow those relating to the spiritual realms. How is it possible to build a resplendent future on a decayed present? Can an unclean mind and diseased body foster a pure and radiant soul?

When a child begins to question its parents concerning its origin, such inquiries are usually avoided or untruthfully answered. The perturbed, thoughtless, morally-ignorant mother or father attribute birth to "the stork," the doctor, the drug store or to some kind fairy, and hastily changes the subject. Can there be greater injury inflicted on a confiding soul than this: deceiving the child? Is it not appalling to consider the foundationless falsehoods impressed upon the young child's mind by its ignorant parents at the very dawn of its intellectual unfoldment?

The degradation of sex has its beginning right here; it will soon be old enough to suspect, and seldom forgets the story told it by the parents. Through companions equally ignorant, it shortly is informed, in the most degrading manner, of the bald, vulgar aspect of the physical contact of the sexes and its results, and the heretofore unsullied mind becomes contaminated with filth, never to be restored to its pristine state. The veracity of the parents is henceforth doubted; the child naturally concludes they were ashamed of the creative act which called it into existence; it treasures to itself the great secret; its active imagination pictures the intimacy of human beings and there is but one result: that child, before its reasoning faculties have fully unfolded, is convinced that the method of creation must be secret, impure, unholy, and an unclean act; something to be ashamed of, veiled in falsehoods. This condition, deplorable as it undoubtedly is, would not be so utterly hopeless, *if it ended here;* but it does not; the corruption of thought and desire appeals to the lowest in the child nature, nurturing a hothouse growth of passionate desire at an age when the urge of sex should be unknown, and the mind be yet thoroughly imbued with stories of fairies and fanes, gods and goddesses of fairy lands.

Secret vice quickly follows the broken faith in loved ones and the information obtained through vulgar companions. Ignorance of a law does not annul its effect. The indifference to duty, the feeling of shrinking timidity and the ignorance as to the extent of the effect of lies and evasions, do not make parents any the less responsible. Mothers and fathers are no less than criminals if they permit their children to be thrown upon the world untaught and therefore unprepared, to rightly use and control the powers of sex. An effect is always the result of a similar cause; if children grow into licentious men and women, if they become debauches and degenerates, finally ending in human wrecks, it surely indicates to the thinking man and woman that there must be a sufficient cause to have produced such an awful result. What food for reflection this offers us who have the improvement of the race at heart as we grasp the significance of the possibilities to the race through the inculcation of the truth, in chaste language, to the children of men!

The intuition of a child is as active, if not more so, than that of the elders; and it therefore senses untruths at an early age. The awakening of reason in the child induces it to ask many questions, undoubtedly awkward to the youthful parents, and every evasion only hinders the child's search for that knowledge which *inherently is its birthright,* and which it has a *right to demand,* and in confidence expect to receive without reservation.

Intuitively the child senses when falsehoods are given it instead of truths in answer to its questions; but is powerless to prevent its reasoning faculties from engendering in its mind the thought that it has been deliberately fooled; yet it cannot comprehend why a lie and evasion is offered it when knowledge is sought. Instinctively he seeks those of, or near, his own age for answers to those questions which continue to force themselves upon his thoughts. Who pays for the *"feeding of stones when bread was asked?"*

Many parents promise themselves that "when the child is older" they will have a "heart-to-heart" talk with it. Even if that resolution is kept and acted upon, it fails to accomplish much good. Before the child is old enough to talk "reasonably" with its parents, school companions, or older people, will already have commenced the demolition of the temple of purity, and the seeds of evil be sown in the mind that might have been kept undefiled. It requires but few insinuations or vile suggestions to produce a turmoil in the imagination of a sensitive child. Besides, there are now, as there always have been, men of the lowest type, who seduce and betray young boys and girls for their own sense-gratification. As an illustration, we cite one case which came under our observation. A boy who had been told the usual falsehood and forbidden to ask further questions, and whose seven years of life had failed to divulge the why and wherefore of his creation and existence, was thrown much into the companionship of a male creature past sixty years of age who had been introduced into the family as a permanent guest. The house being small, the child shared a bed with the old man, who slowly, but surely, taught it all manner of vice whereby his own degenerate desires might be gratified. Ignorant of the right and the wrong, the boy was as clay in the hands of a master potter. Warned to keep silent by the fiend, and fearing his parents, the degenerating habits fastened themselves upon him; with the result that at twelve years of age he was a physical wreck and brought to us for treatment. We obtained the whole foul story; found him fully developed, sexually, at twelve years. His entire nervous system was shattered; vision defective; had pronounced night losses, the brain affected. Here was a human wreck well on the road to a premature grave, at an age when he should have been reading fairy tales. The parents were speechless when confronted with the truth, though loathe to confess that they were the ones most guilty. Pitiable, you exclaim! Admittedly so, but *there are thousands upon thousands of just such cases developing continually, as the result of neglect and ignorance on the part of the parents.* Every form of vice "stalks abroad" seeking youthful victims, and parents not only leave open every avenue, but *invite the catastrophe.* Referring to the case under discussion, it may be of interest to add that after a long period of treatment: moral, mental, and physical, this boy gradually regained his health and became a respectable member of society; but all faith in his parents was gone; through a fault not his own, he had lost that feeling of tender and intimate companionship, kindness, and love for men; and throughout life the inner self of that man will carry the ugly scars inflicted upon him in his youth through the neglect of his parents.

The so-called innate goodness of a child cannot be depended upon to protect it from the influence of vice. As a race, human beings are impregnated with perversions. From time immemorial the very atmosphere surrounding humanity has been saturated with thought-images of sex evils; and it is an exceptional case when the uninstructed, though innocent child, escapes the general contamination. Children are imaginative and imitative; possessing an inherent desire to expand their lives; gain experience and obtain information. Witness how the ordinary child in school beams with pleasure over the acquirement of some special knowledge, or the details of some unusual event. It hastens home to pour into the ears of its mother every new discovery. Especially is this true if that knowledge or event is in any way related to his own particular sensation or enjoyment. If to this supposed knowledge is added the idea of secrecy, the child mind is enthralled. Is there any wonder, then, that sex, as a mysterious, secret, supposed plaything, enslaves it?

The carnal thoughts and destructive habits of past ages are inbred in the child nature of the present generation; the sex desires are hungers of the physical being; and, as the physical nature in man is supreme, it logically follows that these *desires, appetites, and cravings* make themselves felt in the child mind with the first awakening of the sex forces. Consequently, instead of the innate goodness in the boy and girl acting as a protective force, this inborn appetite of the creative energy, impels it to seek ways and means for self-gratification without a thought as to the result to itself or to others. If it does reason, it is thus: *"All those I know are practicing thus and so, seemingly enjoying it, and apparently deriving no ill-effects from it, why should not I do likewise?"* The result is, it does like the rest of its companions and pays the same penalty—a gradual degeneracy of body, mind, and that higher potency in man we term the soul.

What is the remedy? Seek to learn the truth respecting all that concerns sex, and when your children commence to question you, follow your love instinct and tell them the *whole* truth, clothing it in words such as only mother-love can command. Let it be something like in this story-form:

"As you see this great world about you, with its many men, women and children, its green trees, beautiful flowers, birds and animals, so is there another world in the distant beyond which the eyes of the body cannot behold. In that great other world

there are many souls; that you may be better able to understand
what souls are, we will call them children who have neither
father nor mother, and who are more like good fairies; because
in that home they cannot think or do anything wicked, but only
those things which little children do who love their mothers.   In
that home, instead of mothers, there are good women, angels,
who constantly watch over these little children.   We call these
good women their guardian angels; these come to earth with the
children when they come here.

"These little souls, or children, though having everything
they seem to desire, cannot know either pleasure or pain; they
cannot know what it is to love a mother, or to be loved by one,
because they possess no body such as we do, with which to feel,
laugh or cry, and run to its mother when in trouble.

"In time, as they see the children on earth romp and play,
among themselves or with animal pets, in their garden of flowers,
with their little stubbed toes, mothers caressing and kissing
their babies; seeing them retire to sleep, mothers listening to
their prayers and fondly tucking them in their little beds, these
little souls of the other world become dissatisfied with their
heaven and long to become as other little children, even though
they may stub their toes, become sick, have pain and be made to
cry; as well as having nice things to play with, and good things
to eat, with mother loving and kissing them.   This longing in
the hearts of these little souls gradually opens the way for them
to come to this earth, so that they may have bodies like you and
other children; but before they can come here, a place to receive
them must be carefully prepared.

"Within your mother, God, who is the Father of the heaven
from which, and to which, all good fairies and souls belong, and
from which your father and mother came, has prepared a little
temple which is to receive such little souls as wish to come to
earth.   In this little temple within mother, your father who loves
her, and who desired a little child to love, sowed a tiny seed
and gradually this began to grow.   After a long time this seed
within the temple of mother began to look like a little child, then

one day it was ready to leave the little temple and come forth, to be as other children.

"Now, all this time, while this little body was growing, you, a fairy soul in that other world, dissatisfied with your home there, were wishing to come to earth. Your guardian angel, always with, or near you, carefully watched so that nothing might happen to you, and prepared for the long trip from Fairy-land to the Earth-home, where father and mother, and the little body in the temple, were waiting for you. Then one day, the glad tidings came that the body, the little house which you were to enter, would soon be ready. Your guardian angel prepared all the things which belonged to you and had you all ready for the time when the call should come. At last came the day when you were told by the guardian angel to bid good-bye to all your companions and be ready to commence the journey. As you traveled from the land of Souls and Fairies, you quickly noted a change; whereas in your former home it was warm and you could feel neither pain or pleasure, you now approached a place where it was cold and you felt like crying. But you had little time to think, or to change your mind; you saw your mother who seemed to be very much larger than you thought she would be; this almost frightened you; yet you were fascinated by your surroundings and your attention was held by the Guardian Angel who told you to be ready to meet your mother.

"Very soon the door of the temple was opened, though it seemed to you that mother suffered great pain; and you beheld coming from this temple, which God had built in mother, a little body just like many you had so often seen in the arms of other mothers while you were yet in Fairyland. Your guardian Angel told you to be ready as this was to be your home, and that with the first cry from the body you would fall asleep; and when you awoke you would feel heavy and cold, and would be hungry, and crying for the warm feeling which you had always known. Suddenly you became unconscious, and seemed to sleep for a long time; when you awoke everything seemed dark and cold; you heard yourself cry and did not know what to do because you could no longer move from place to place by simply wishing, as formerly. You called upon your guardian Angel; but, though you could see her, she seemed to be at a distance and could not help you as she had been able to before. Soon they washed and dressed you and you found yourself in mother's arms; you soon felt warm and found yourself gradually sinking into a peaceful sleep. You could still perceive your guardian Angel; but as you came to know more of your mother, you could see less of your guardian Angel, until now you no longer see her, though she is still watching over you as she did in that far-off Fairy-land, and would feel deeply hurt if she saw you do things which displeased mother.

"This is the way all babies come to earth. Mother has told you this but it is not well for you to speak of it to other children as they might not understand. Let it be a secret between you and your mother; and when other children wish to talk with you about these things, tell them only father and mother can understand them.

This is the truth as sacred philosophy teaches us; in language the child can grasp. To be sure, it may be clothed in varied forms, but in it is contained the answer to the oft propounded question: "Mother, where did I come from?" If the one questioned has the true mother instinct, the mother love, she need not hesitate to tell the story to her child no matter what its age. If all mothers would answer their children honestly and without reservation, inviting their confidence and further questions, telling them not to listen to the stories voiced by other children, the basic foundation would be laid for a life that would know no shame.

Is this desirable and worth the effort? Then let parents tell their children the truth and nothing but the truth; and one generation hence we will have abolished much of the ignorance and degeneracy so prevalent today.

We refuse to believe the future will continue to produce the selfish, narrow-minded, ignorant, prudish parents of the present generation; because there are men and women, ministers, teachers, writers, physicians, and lawyers, who have dedicated themselves to this movement of sex enlightenment and exaltation of the Creative function. These are thinking men and women who are ready to assume the place and responsibility of parents, helping to save many of the children of the present generation.

Because of the prejudice of the masses, and even many of the classes, the work will of necessity be hindered and many children be prevented from receiving much-needed instruction; but the night of ignorance will be illuminated with understanding, thereby helping future generations; and if all who but dimly perceive the light will *do their best,* the great work of race improvement, through the teaching of sex truths, will be spread. The morn of a better day is dawning.

The Great Madness

"This stuff taught the innocent girl that, when a man doffs his hat to her, rises in her presence, etc., he is expressing innate respect for noble womanhood, is piffle, according to the feminists.

"Only the harem woman wants men to commit these so-called gallantries," says Margaret Hatfield, Smith College graduate, former Hull House worker.

"The tired business man finds them a nuisance. So does the self-respecting woman. They are regarded as special privileges granted women. How can a woman who demands full equality consistently accept them?

"In the eyes of the law Margaret Hatfield is merely the wife of Stuart Chase, who is prominently associated with the Federal Trade Commission, and the mother of two children.

"I refuse to be an erased identity, therefore I retain my maiden name," she says, "I weakly submitted to changing it on marriage. I cried on my wedding night at the thought of giving it up. When I declared my independence, I took it back. I have also eliminated the prefix 'Miss.' It comes from the German 'fraulein,' which means womanlet. I am neither a womanlet nor a submerged personality."—*The Evening Bulletin, Philadelphia, October 20, 1920.*

Despite all the destructive and demoralizing bombastic utterances of fossils in the shape of either males or females, we maintain, *as does every true man and woman*, that man doffs his hat to woman, rises in her presence, and attempts to appear at his best, because of his respect for womanhood, and also, *due to the image in his heart and mind of an Ideal woman, a remnant of the old chivalry inherited from his ancestors when women still believed in virtue and the sacredness of her sex, and when she taught her daughters to so think and act as to demand respect from man, while she instructed her sons in the precepts of clean-liness of mind and body and the godliness of being a gentleman.*

The harem woman does *not* look for these gallantries, she is well satisfied if she, being merely one out of many, receives a kind word now and then. But the educated and refined woman expects the *all* that one man can give her, and the respect of the others. To *be denied these is to be condemned as beneath notice.*

It is utterly false, as a universal vote would quickly prove, that complying with the rules of politeness are considered a nuis-ance by the business man. On the contrary, no one is quicker to sense when deference is due to a woman and none more will-ingly offers homage. Admittedly, the successful business man with his ability to read human nature unconsciously, is quick to sense when he meets the sexually dormant female of a new specie, and willingly complies with her unvoiced wishes not to render her respect—respect and gallantries *are* synomonous.

We maintain absolutely, without any reservation whatever, that every clean-hearted, virgin-minded, self-respecting woman *does* look for the respect of every man with whom she comes in contact, while the worth while women of America, the mothers of the men who are to do the big things, are proud of the privi-lege of bearing some man's good name. If they are not, then it is exceptionally safe to say they do not really love the husband; in which case we say without hesitation, accepting the Bible as authority, that they are living in wedded prostitution with the man whose name they do not respect.

Consider the mental attitude of a woman who marries, and through that act is supposed to uncontradictably confess that she loves the man who is to be life's partner, confessing that on her wedding night she cried because she had to give up her maiden name. Think of her entering the bridal chamber and complying with the wishes of her husband in what should be the most sacred relationship known to man, while her thoughts are antagonistic to the laws governing the embrace! Is it any wonder the nation is now honeycombed with sexless, masculine women, and effeminate men?

Cardinal Gibbons, Rabbi Krauskopf, and other noted churchmen deplore the present destructive and demoralizing trend of the age, but have they the strength, and the courage, to boldly proclaim against the prostitution of the marital relationship by feminists, self-lovers, homo-sexualists, and Henry Pecks—and terming it properly—the basic cause of the world upheaval?

How can the churchmen of the world reconcile their religious inculcation, their ordination to the ministry, their knowledge of the sacred edict "to thy husband shalt be thy thought" with the many present day feminist movements, all of which are destructive to the home, therefore to the state, consequently to the nation, lastly to the entire race? We, appointed to God's ministry through direct apostolic descension, would feel our Soul cursed by God if we did not boldly proclaim against the *Great Madness* and uphold, with all the strength of our being, the sacredness of the marriage rite, the glory of motherhood, the innocence of womanhood, and the necessity for the respect and gallantries of noble manhood toward all true womanhood.

Instruction for the Girl

Of the many who have soiled reams of perfectly clean paper with dissertations on the waywardness of the girl, few have dared to honestly seek the cause and to voice the result of their wholehearted investigations. Questions without number have been propounded; among them such as: "Why do girls allow themselves to be led astray?" "Why do our girls, seemingly deliberately, choose the wrong path, knowing, as they surely must, the difference between right and wrong; the status of the "fallen" woman; aware through instinct and education, that the virtuous maiden has infinitely greater chances to marriage and happiness than the one whose name has become sullied."

Seldom does it occur to the questioner that a correct understanding of herself and proper training would most assuredly have been the means of preventing a wrong choice; that had the girl actually appreciated the value of the sex impulse; having been instructed in the nature of the desire and incentive to mate, she would be protected, not only against the men who woo, but likewise against her own carnal inclinations.

Undoubtedly uncountable mothers of exceptional character and broadmindedness are at a loss how to instruct their daughters. It is their heart's desire to have the girl remain pure and innocent; yet do not wish to suppress the charm of the maiden, nor dull the vivacity native to the healthy young.

Evil is relative. There are many degrees in the so-called "fall" of women. A girl may go astray, yet be truly virtuous at heart; she may leave the path of virtue and become a woman of ill repute; or may live a life of evil because of inherited destructive tendencies. The motive and the cause must ever enter into consideration of the individual case. An untold number of girls, having made a mistake, recognize it, reconstruct their lives and take their place in respectable society; these often become the best wives and mothers. Others, a heartbreaking number of them, follow the downward path until disease, then friendly death finally claims them.

Contrary to the general opinion, there are conditions in life more to be feared than loss of innocence; secret, morbid, soul-destroying solitary vices infinitely worse than the performance of sex embrace outside the pale of matrimony. For those who ignore the moral code there is every hope of reform and a useful, constructive life; but the girl who falls a victim of unnatural acts and desires is almost universally incapable of becoming a satisfactory, or satisfied, wife and mother; the moral fibre having undergone a form of disintegration, imbecility and recurrence of habits, ending in degeneration.

Two special reasons may be advanced for the downfall of the majority of women: Love and money. In ninety per cent of all cases it is safe to claim the first step was taken as the result of affection, or the emotion most human beings mistake for love. As the girl nears womanhood, she becomes conscious of a desire to love and be loved; she is aware of the awakening within herself of the most divine of all passions; that of offering herself on the altar of love. Women universally are far different from the male specie; she deifies the object of her love, generously bestowing upon him every god-like quality; is easily persuaded that her love must be proved to the uttermost. Her motive is pure; she is actuated by impulses as old as mankind, though even today but dimly understood. It is impossible for some natures to comprehend they are committing sin when they consent "for love's sake."

Many women, possessed of highly-organized religious natures, deify their love; their emotion of love becoming personified. A proof of such deification and personification is had in Gasgrain's *"Vie de Marie de l' Incarnation."* This Marie of the confession is willing to offer life itself that her desire for divine love may be fulfilled. She confesses: "Going to prayer, I trembled in myself and exclaimed, 'Let us go into a solitary place, my dear love, that I may embrace you, at my ease, and that, breathing my soul into you, it may be but yourself only, in the union of love. Oh, my love, when shall I embrace you? Have you no pity on me in the torments that I suffer? Alas, alas, my love, my beauty, my life! instead of healing my pain, you take pleasure in it. Come, let me embrace you, and die in your sacred arms.' Then, as I was spent with fatigue, I was forced to say: My divine love, since you wish me to live, I pray you let me rest a little, that I may better serve you,' and I promised him that afterward I would suffer myself to consume in his chaste and divine embrace."

We have personally received the confession of many women, highly respected in their communities, who, *destructively frigid in their sex relationship with their husbands*, would attend religious revival meetings, and, having their emotions aroused through the hectic, and often fanatic, sermons; and the expressed, verbal and by motion, emotions of the congregation, would *pass through the sensual-nervous crisis* as does the normal, healthy woman in embrace with her husband; and on her return home to her "lord and master," be as cold and virtuous (?), toward him, as ever. However, in this department of our work we are dealing with the normal, healthy young woman who is capable of loving and desirous of receiving it; not with the emotionalism of the hectic, erotic, fanatical religious, unbalanced-minded class.

Every mother is aware, if she has given the subject any thought whatever, that sex-awakening must come to her daughter; aye, it being desirable that it should. She cannot fail to remember her own thoughts and desires during the days of her youth; this assuring her that intimate sex knowledge is essential to the life of *every real woman*. The gradual process of the development from innocent maidenhood to desired womanhood, with its unfoldment and possibilities must not be accepted as a condition to be suppressed, crushed, ignored, or clothed with apology. It is not unholy, nor unnatural, *quite the opposite;* for no greater blessing was ever bestowed upon woman than this most holy and desirable emotion of seeking *to be possessed.* It is a Divine, deific promise, given in advance, of her value to the race of real men; and through this sex impulse she may add to the sum total of human happiness; become a channel for the birth of superior human creatures, thereby hastening her own evolution; or she may bring misery to herself and her progeny; delaying her own progress toward perfection. The results are always in exact ratio with what she has been taught as the truth, and her obedience thereto.

Mothers dare no longer shrink from the positive duty they owe their daughters. The origin, nature, and effect of sex emotion and indulgence must be fully, sanely, and elevationally explained; evasions and innuendoes are destructive. When the girl receives enlightenment on both the cause and satisfaction of her emotions, she will possess the weapon of knowledge.

The fear that an open discussion over-reaches the desired results, that the young are induced by curiosity to investigate hidden paths after they have been instructed, is not a sane and logical argument. The subject denuded of its false, ingenuous, secret aspect; presented in a normal, unprejudiced manner, will do much to curb undue interest. The beautiful, desirable, and constructive, as well as the hideous, damning, and destructive phases, must all have consideration. Knowledge may add intensity to the girl's nature, but innate goodness, fortified with understanding, will be an incentive for her to follow the right. *Girls are naturally pure in thought and desire;* will not be led to ruin through knowledge; ignorance alone is to be feared.

One manifestation of the feminine sex nature (often the direct cause of the girl's undoing), scarcely, if ever, given the serious consideration it deserves, is the *instinctive, inborn,* mother-love nature, the inheritance of *every* female. The moment the true woman loves, at that instant does she begin to serve. It is her innate nature inducing a longing in her to supply all the wants of the loved one, whether of a social, mental, or physical type. His comfort and well-being become her aim in life, and if uninstructed, the whisperings of her conscience will scarcely be heard and certainly avail nothing as against his pleadings. He appears restless and anhungered, she readily offers herself—an unconscious (until too late) sacrifice. The call of sex desire in her, though playing a part, is not the actual reason for her compliance with his request; the mother-love, desire-to-be-possessed, is. The ideal wife is half mother to the object of her love; she serves her husband as though he were a child; grants all his favors; whether demanded in or out of season. A thorough explanation of this infinitely varied side of her nature must be offered the girl, thus guarding her against an unwise sacrifice as proof of her love.

The actual purposes and usages of her creative nature are not understood by one girl in each thousand; generally all the information the many possess being gained from unreliable sources; from companions as ignorant of the saving facts as themselves. Because of this undesirable condition, the great need to prevent the multitude of innocent girls being led astray, or into love unions, or what *appear* as love-unions, blindfolded, is sane, sensible, thorough instructions and training. Girls are best reached through the mother; boys through the father; fathers and mothers must be taught the laws and powers, uses and abuses, of sex. *Above all, the penalty resultant of disobeying these sex laws, either through ignorance or choice, fully inculcated.* When fathers and mothers are imbued with the divinity of all of God's creation,—no department is more sublime than this one through which He makes us co-creators with Him,— when they realize this sublimity and harmonize it with knowledge, they are then in a position to free the path that their young may walk in and be protected. So long as parents possess only the sensational, crude, vulgar, and distorted conceptions and information obtained during their own youth; while they believe this important subject is to be discussed in a veiled, obscure, secretive manner, and ridicule and condemn public education; just that long will they, *the parents, be blameworthy and held accountable, for the sins and the shame and the suffering of their progeny.*

Until the time of the great war the public considered it

criminal, and contrary to morality, to inculcate sex truths; despite the fact that the lack of knowledge was the prolific cause of the existing evils. Think of it! *The twentieth century, yet men and women, arrested, fined, or imprisoned for attempting to light the lamp of knowledge that would shed light on a subject, which, because of the ignorance concerning it, has been the cause of destroying whole nations! Men and women, at the instigation of a moral leper named Comstock, branded as criminals, cast into prison, there committing suicide, because they dared teach the truth on a sacred subject, in a chaste manner!* God pity men for their stupendous arrogance and ignorance, for their colossal egotism!

The time is not far distant when this deplorable condition will be entirely reversed. Men will be held responsible for the education and enlightenment of their families; be considered criminals if they neglect their sacred duty; and shall be punished severely for the proved ignorance of their children.

What opinion would be entertained of the man or woman who presented the boy or girl with an intricate mechanism, compelling the child to make use of it, yet withholding knowledge of its operation? Suppose that machine combined both life-giving and death-dealing qualities, and the giver refused to offer any instructions for its operation and the protection of the person, would we not rightly feel abhorrence toward him and seek his incarceration? As a further illustration, imagine this same parent keeping guard over the helpless child, having builded a wall termed "parental authority" about it, menacing the competent men and women without who were pleading for the privilege of instructing the child in the operation of the potent instrument. Is it not an appalling picture?

If the modern enlightened mother were informed her daughter possessed some great talent, would she urge the girl to dedicate it to the devil, having been informed that sin, sickness, misery and death were the consequences? On the contrary, would she not rejoice and help to develop the desirable gift, uplifting and praising, so bringing joy, power, health, and beauty to the daughter she loved?

Would one willingly allow one's children to play with a viper? Would not the heart contract with horrible fear at the thought of its fangs and poison? Despite the conjured picture, uncountable careless, ignorant parents, brutally indifferent, close their eyes to plain, uncontradictable facts, leaving their children to the malignant influences of ignorance, more deadly than the fangs of the viper for that can only destroy the body; then, with breaking hearts bewail their fate, and impeach the Father of All-good, when a daughter enters a brothel instead of a home; or becomes the mother of an unnamed child; or suffers lingering death from some loathsome disease. *Who, at the great accounting,* will be adjudged guilty, and suffer the greater punishment? Surely not the child born and raised in ignorance.

The basis of sex instruction should be its *holiness*. There is naught degrading in passion. The only profane phase is the destructive thought of prejudiced, ignorant humanity, and the ignoble purpose to which sex is condemned. It is insufficient to preach of the swift penalty following debasement of the creative function; the pure, exalted, sacred purpose must be enlarged upon. The possibilities for good or evil of the generative organism must be minutely taught; while exposing the dark, secret, and destructive usages of which humanity is guilty.

Parents and teachers must search their own hearts for the slightest trace of impurity of thought. Many who are today invaluable as teachers and leaders in the enlightening movement learned their lessons after reaching maturity, or through great personal suffering and the consequent adjustment. All these, as with one voice, maintain the necessity of purity in thought; youth being psychically expert in sensing the least hint of shame, or the feeling of self-consciousness.

Of the many false conceptions respecting sex and its functions, that of repression is the most destructive and degrading. It has been impressed, more by inference than by actual words, that woman is coarse and unwomanly if she allows sex desires to manifest; leading them to believe they should possess no feeling; that if they are passionate it should be thoroughly controlled and denied, being an inheritance to be ashamed of. These victims of the goddess of ignorance, actually believe it unrighteous and unbecoming to display any emotion, even in embrace with their husbands, deeming it an ideal state to appear as a mere machine; giving all, receiving nothing in return. This idea of passivity of sex in women is well-nigh universal; from it may be traced ninety per cent of the degrading practice of one class of women, and the so-called female weakness of the other. We know whereof we speak; soul-despairing confessions having supplied us with the knowledge. The greater pity of it is, these suffering women often become the mothers of daughters.

Woman has every right to as great an enjoyment as man; God gave passion equally to the male and the female; therefore the coldness resultant of repression is unnatural. Under no circumstances should natural desires be denied and repressed and its possession considered with shame. True, passion should be mastered; controlled until the proper time for right expression. Repression is the path to abnormal physical and emotional conditions; and continued, gives birth to degraded and perverted desires, or destruction of the creative power.

Many males, incorrectly termed men, subscribe to the theory that women should repress, then proceed to condemn them for being cold; these have not yet reached the degree of enlightenment where they are willing to grant equality; have not arrived at an understanding of the necessity of passion in women. These men still remain in bondage to the past and consider it immodest for women to meet them with sincere feeling, demanding an equal exchange.

Girls must be taught that normal, controlled sex power is forever creative; if not abused, but rightly controlled and diffused throughout the body, it is the basis of strength and beauty of body, and brilliancy of mind. The perfection of her form, the smoothness, loveliness, and texture of her skin, the sweetness of her voice, and the fire of her eyes, all depend on, and are due to, this creative potency.

When the girl comprehends that every part of her nature is God's gift to her to be used according to His law, she will rejoice in her possessions and nothing will be able to tempt her to debase them, nor will she do ought that may cheapen herself in any manner. She must be brought to the comprehension that unnatural repression, trying to root out, or kill any desire or function, is equally as wrong as the misuse. Her sole duty is to be mistress of herself; to control the passion that at times rise and surge within her, until such time she meets the right mate who will prove his love by contracting a partnership with her through Holy wedlock.

Questions often propounded: "What are we to do with our daughters when they pass the dividing line between girlhood and womanhood, possessed of an abundance of life, and love, and creative instinct, how help them to control their desires?"

The first requisite is to keep the mind fully occupied with duties to be performed, or problems to be solved. So long as they are wholeheartedly interested in work and play, they are safe. Treat the girls as we do the boys; boys are active creatures and free themselves of excessive energy by work and athletics. Allow the girl to romp and be a tom-boy to her heart's content; you will never find the seed of sex trouble as long as she does. When that age and stage is past, she must be induced to find interest in some task or practice. Work given her must be neither monotonous nor confining; change is essential; as is time spent in the open air; and in whatever she centers her mind she must be continually encouraged; it is imperative she have an *incentive* to act.

Admittedly, not all girls can be guided in this manner. In the quiet, sedentary, studious, the pursuit most interesting to them should be encouraged; while the more active physical exercises should not be forced upon them. Music, painting, the arts, whatever they can be interested in, should be indulged; care being exercised that the fancy does not lead toward the morbid.

Interest is the key. Instruct the girl in the laws governing sex, then keep her interested and the entire problem finds a solution of itself. The moment a girl becomes dissatisfied, the danger signal is hoisted.

The duty of every mother is apparent; she must devote as close attention to the development of her daughter as the father **does to business.** A man pays close attention to every detail of his vocation, studies continuously how to combat certain influences; how to remedy leakages and deficits; is eternally vigilant. The mother's daughter is *her* business, and she must apply herself in like manner. If all is not as it should be, *seek the cause;* change occupation, plans, and recreation; be deft in the art of substitution.

Far too often the normal, healthy, vivacious, active girl is deprived of necessary innocent pleasures. She wishes to visit a friend, attend the theatre, witness a game, go on a picnic, or attend a party. These innocent pastimes are refused her; she is *thrown back upon herself; trouble brews,* and a deplorable situation quickly develops. Her mind becomes resentful; seeking an outlet for the dammed-up energy; imagination commences to play; and if evil companions or blase stories have previously opened the way, *the devil steps in.* The average, developing girl is not expected to set aside all pleasure; noble, elevating thoughts alone will not sustain her at this period of her life. Pleasure constantly denied, solitary vice, or secret meetings with the undesirable of the opposite sex, are likely to be the result.

The solution of the problem is found in:

1. Teaching the girl the creative laws in detail and frankness; presenting every side clearly, especially dwelling on all that is beautiful, fascinating, beneficial, and constructive to herself and the race. Invite questions and reply without hesitation, in chaste language and without self-consciousness. Praise her (within reason) to assist her in a correct valuation of herself. Be her friend and confidant.

2. Supply her with work of an interesting nature. Dwell much on the honor of housekeeping and motherhood. Temporary employment about the house to become proficient in housekeep-

ing, or preliminary training for a vocation, are highly desirable. Encourage the development of any apparent talent. Do not allow her to become one-sided and impracticable; and unless a girl has positive genius, it is better to encourage her to do well several things. The sensible, adaptable woman becomes the best wife and mother.

3. Exercise is one of the essentials. Any method, if constructive, is desirable. Games furnish it—tennis, rowing, walking are highly important. If these do not suffice or appear unsuitable, arrange for regular gymnastic work. The object is to keep the body agile, the blood in active circulation, and the creative forces distributed.

4. Amusements are as important as exercise. All pleasure should combine harmless recreation with elevating tendencies. It is questionable whether any but the most esthetic girls could remain normal and free from vice without sufficient amusements.

Girls seek the downward path because their requirements are neither recognized nor provided for by their natural guardians. Parents fail in their duty and this neglect cannot be corrected in after life. During the formative period girls learn of matters concerning sex, and more often it is the degrading conception rather than an elevating comprehension of the influence and potency of the functions and forces. Once imbued with these ideas, she becomes incapable of either understanding, or gaining, true love; consequently she is condemned to live on the husks of affection.

Parents generally seem to make but little effort to understand their daughters; their feelings, likes and dislikes; their inclinations, weaknesses, and strength. They urge them to accomplish either too much, or too little; allow them no amusements at all, cr satiate their desires by overdoing. A sane, balanced, intelligent parent is a God-send, an angel of mercy, to any child. Let us hope for more such in the near future.

The girl of the present is an independent creature and it is unwise to either suspect her motives, or accuse her of indiscretions, nor to impute wrong to mere folly and inexperience. Parents should be certain before attempting any accusations and even then the methods employed should be corrective and sympathetic.

Chiding, scolding, and threatening, is so much wasted energy. Love your daughters into obedience of instructions and counsel rather than commanding them; humans can more often be loved into goodness, than punished into it. Have faith in your daughter; trust her; be her companion and partner; forget her mistakes; keep forever before her mind the fact that she is a flower in the Garden of Man; that God expects her to retain her sweetness and purity.

When the girl goes estray, *place the blame where it rightly belongs.* The guilty one is not always the inexperienced, frail little woman-flower, but the ignorant parents, *and those in authority who prohibit the inculcation of sex truths.*

Continence in the Unmarried

At first glance, the continent life, in its relation to the un-married, apparently is an extremely simple proposition, but in giving the problem serious consideration, it assumes appalling proportions, especially as one is confronted with the various com-plicated aspects in its relation to different temperaments and men and women of age from youth to dotage.

Unquestionably we prescribe the continent life for the single, whether man or woman, irrespective of age, color, creed, or clime; in so doing we fearlessly accept the absolute truth and consider both its desirability and ill effects.

Many writers recognized internationally as authorities and whose conclusions are accepted without question, based their deductions on the laws governing animal life and action; how-ever, it is extremely doubtful if these men and women have ever lived outside the city limits, and some of them would possibly have difficulty in recognizing the difference between the male and female in certain of the animal specie.

Had these people completed their knowledge by a domicile in the country for a few years, surrounded by horses, cows, and other animals, they would be extremely wary of basing their conclusions on animal habits and practices. Why? Because those of us who have appealed to Nature for first-hand information relative to animal life, *have witnessed, time and again, and therefore know,* that the stallion, the bull, the goat, as well as other animals, constantly practice masturbation after reaching a certain age; so pronounced does this habit become that breeders often have resource to saltpetre, therewith to reduce the passion-ate nature of these animals, thus checking the practice.

This is undoubtedly an ugly truth to express, but one, gen-erally understood, will necessitate many accepted authorities to seek in other than realms of the animal kingdom, upon which to base their instructions dealing with sex practices.

Having thus disputed one of the foundations whereon many writers founded their entire theory in dealing with sexual hygiene, we will consider another, namely, Nature.

Practically all teachers of the subject who did not form their conclusions on what they believe to be the laws and habits governing the animal kingdom, did so on their understanding of Nature's laws, telling us that it is natural for man to live the continent life while remaining single. This inference is as erroneous as the first, because the law governing throughout all the realms of creative nature, is: *As soon as sentient creatures reach the age where reproduction is possible, they mate, cohabit regularly in season; being governed exclusively by their instincts; and many, in fact, most animals are decidedly polygamic.* Moreover, Nature does not question whether reproduction really does result, and it is an actual fact that in numerous instances, especially with finely bred animals, it is necessary to mate them time and again before conception does occur.

Thus, throughout the domain of Nature instinct and season alone is recognized. There is absolutely no code of morality or of honor governing; and the only law obeyed is: *Use the function and forces of reproduction just as soon as they are sufficiently developed, and continue their exercise, whenever possible, until age ends all.*

This is the fiat of Nature and decidedly no more desirable for humanity to obey than the instincts governing animal life and inciting them to action. A comprehension and acceptation of these facts will urge us to seek deeper for a rule of action which is applicable to mankind and in harmony with God's great purpose.

What then is this Law?

Simply this: Man is dual in his nature. First, the animal or creative instinct governing his desires and which he generally obeys. In fact, few ever gain the knowledge and strength to wisely rule the function.   Possibly this is well, otherwise creation might cease.

Second, the Divine inheritance—a consciousness giving man the right of choice.   Knowing and feeling the urge of his human and animal nature, he possesses a mind with which he can control the desires of his lower nature.

Concisely stated, this infers that at the dictation of his Divine nature, he exercises the creative, or animal, function only when his higher self indicates that it is best for him so to do. We say "best" advisably, because the code of morality changes from age to age, and what is believed right in this day may be considered totally wrong in the near future.   This is clearly indicated in the Biblical stories wherein acts recorded would today be pronounced as criminal, but in the time of their consummation were blessed of God, because necessary to the continuation of the race.

Since neither the instincts which govern the action of animals, nor the laws of Nature, as generally understood, are applicable to the action of enlightened men, we base our conclusions and instructions on the indisputable fact that man is an *accountable being;* possessing the privilege of *free choice;* that within him are two entirely separate personalities; one governed by Natural Law and Animal Desire; the other by the Divine Prompting of God; *maintaining throughout that this Higher Law should govern his creative acts;* permitting exercise of the function only when to the best interests of humanity, himself, and God's great Purpose.

Almost from the moment of birth there is an urge in the creature, whether animal or human, to exercise the creative function, and as days pass into weeks, weeks into months, months into years, this incitant, with the awakening of desire, continues to increase in intensity until by the time adolescence craving for indulgence is well nigh uncontrollable.

This is comprehensible when we are aware that only because of it is the world populated; were it not for this uncontrolled longing, the knowledge of pain following the birth of a new creature, would induce practically all in the feminine world to refuse the union which results in a new creation. The constant urge and desire to exercise the creative function, is, as we have said, Nature's law for her own protection; and it must be admitted, still governs the majority of mankind.

No effort is required on the part of anyone to have this inherent craving for sexual indulgence increase with the bodily growth; it is Mother Nature herself within the bosom of the creature, so that it shall become a co-creator with Her.

All this is indisputable, and is readily proven by the well-known fact that we find among children of the most tender years, both male and female, those who practice abuse and continue it until either weakness or death, knowledge of undesirable results, or marriage, induces them to discontinue.

The child is a product of Nature and develops harmoniously with her laws, which infers that it inherits the strength and the vices of the animal kingdom, with all its tendencies; there being no need to instruct it in practices which belong to both the animal and natural realms, *it is an inherent cell-consciousness.*

As previously mentioned, within the animal body with its animal instinct, there is an inherent potency not possessed by the rest of the animal creation; *this we term the Divine Principle.* Generally this is dormant in all children, and may remain so during all of life; the natural and animal natures being allowed to govern every action.

Here we have the *key* to the entire problem. It indicates a method for the instruction of the youth, through obedience of which he will be enabled to live the continent life and set aside, for the time being, both natural and animal laws, and thus reap a great benefit, rather than a weakness.

This desirable result is possible only through a systematic course of instruction and training; thereby arousing the Divine nature in the youth; having it keep pace with the development of the creative animal nature, meanwhile controlling it. This is not as difficult as one might suppose, though it unquestionably requires self-control and denial.

The method necessitates the thorough instruction of every youth in all creative laws, moral codes, and his own Divine possibilities; the inculcation of a thorough understanding of the purposes of the creative organism and the correct exercise of the function for but three principle purposes, namely: Reproduction; Re-creation, or the reconstruction of the self being, and Regeneration.

Merely teaching the youths these laws would not be sufficient any more than locking the safety valve in a steam engine would prevent the escape of steam when the pressure became greater than the power of resistence of the boiler. If understanding *and protection* is sought, there must be a thorough knowledge of the power and use of the forces, *as also a natural and divinely accepted method for the use, reabsorption, or transmutation of the superfluous energy.*

We are aware that the man or woman who is given to extremely hard physical labor, to worry, anxiety, severe study, or exercise and training requiring great nerve and muscular force, is, for the time being, practically free from desires of a procreative nature; this clearly points to us a method whereby the functions may be controlled without detrimental effects on the being.

First: Through a careful selection of food, including in the dietary only those articles which contain the maximum amount of nerve, brain, and rebuilding material, and the minimum of stimulating, irritating, and congesting substances; a wise selection of drinks, avoiding those stimulating and depressing, such as tea and coffee; all alcoholic liquors; and so-called "soft" drinks; these latter actually inducing an irritation of the kidneys, having a direct exciting action on the sexual organism; more destructive than beer and light wine, and equally as great as whiskey.

Second: Bathing to cleanse the system of all congestions; keeping the pores of the skin free from poisonous substances, and inducing it to perform its functions of absorbing fresh air.

Third: Careful selection of wearing apparel, choosing for

comfort; not too tight; porous, thus allowing fresh air to reach the skin. Wearing woolen clothing next to the skin is reprehensible and destructive to morals. No condemnation can be too severe of the universal practice of having children and youths wear woolen underwear; this should be countenanced only for the aged, those who have reached senility.

Fourth: Exercise is of vast importance. It not alone develops the body, nerves, and muscles; exhilerating the mind, but it also is inducive to the circulation to "draw up" much of the vital fluids which promote growth; giving incentive to the mind and strengthening the character; thereby greatly lessening the desire for sexual gratification.

Fifth: Association. Possibly nothing else, with the exception of food, has the vast influence on the desires as have associates. Whenever possible, these should be selected from youths of like age, known to be of clean habits and chaste language; also of people much older, capable of giving moral courage, incentive, and a longing for achievement. The cleanest mind and purest heart can quickly be poisoned by continually listening to suggestive word picturing.

Sixth: Recreation. This is essential to the well-being of every boy and girl, and should include games, dramas, motion pictures, and dancing. All games requiring muscular activity and nerve force will help to naturally use up the stored creative energy and at the same time elevate the mind; lifting the thoughts from the physical to the mental and spiritual. All dances, plays, operas, and games suggestive or sex-arousing in their tendency, should be prohibited.

Seventh: Sleep is likewise important; the hours to be carefully regulated, so arranging the time of retiring that it is possible to at once fall asleep; arising immediately after awakening in the morning; followed by a cool bath and physical exercises.

Eighth: Teaching *personal responsibility*. Child and youth should consistently be taught personal responsibility for every act; that a vicarious atonement cannot relieve it of the penalty resultant on non-good act; nor withhold the reward of well-doing. It must be instructed in the function of the creative organism; that the exercise for mere pleasure produces a loss which cannot be replaced and is inducive of weakness and disease; depletion of creative energy, of body, nerves and mind; *directly effecting the Soul itself. This must be relative to religious practices having influence on the Spiritual part of man.*

Ninth: The inculcation of the law that every act and thought having effect on the sexual organism has a direct influence on the mind, and nerves, as also on the Soul; and its future welfare *here and hereafter.* That any drain permitted the creative organism is potent for evil on the mind and soul and lessens the possibility of Immortality; sexual exercise being allowable only in the process of procreation; for the purposes of recreation of the self; and the Re-generation of the Spiritual in man; pleasure being permissible, but secondary.

Tenth: A complete system of breathing exercises which enables one to draw the seminal fluids directly into the circulation, helping in the storing of vital force, mental and nerve power, and Spirituality. This is a direct Regenerative process and enables those who practice it, to avoid suffering from the body, mind, and soul shattering cravings which often overcome the strongest men and women who do not possess this knowledge of transmutation of the forces.

Thus far we have given our consideration only to the youth. Admittedly it is much easier to deal with these than with that other large class composed of men and women who have reached the age of responsibility, but who, for reasons of their own, remain unmarried. With the youth we can begin the correct training at an early age, but with the other class greater difficulties are to be overcome because many of them have always had the wrong perspective of life and action; taught and trained incorrectly, and possibly becoming the victims of destructive habits. Generally the identical methods must be followed by all, irrespective of the age of the individual.

Unquestionably Natural Laws intended that men and women, having passed the period of adolescence, should mate and become sponsors for a family. Early development of the procreative functions and energies indicates this clearly; custom has made this impractical in many instances, though it must be admitted many errors, and vices, would be avoided if youths were to marry soon after they attained manhood and womanhood.

Countless men who might be happily married and the fathers of families are existing in single cussedness through no fault of their own, but because of the ignorance or bigotism of their parents.

We constantly come into touch with men whose mothers have led them to believe the modern woman is not desirable as a wife; no longer in possession of virtue and womanliness; advising them to avoid such women and remain single. In some instances these mothers actually believe what they preach; but in the majority it is purely selfishness because these sons are their sole support.

While we freely admit that man does owe a duty to his parents, nevertheless, his *first* responsibility after reaching manhood's estate, is to seek a mate and become the father of a family, thereby honoring God and his own creative potency.

In proportion to the number of women, possibly not as large a percentage today become good wives and mothers as formerly, nevertheless, there is no dearth in good and virtuous women willing to become wives and mothers. As all of life is more or less of an experiment, no mother is justified in preventing her son from marrying; nor should any man allow fear or cowardice to prevent him from seeking a mate, merely because he may make a mistake.

Life itself is at best an experiment. God allowed man to embody in the flesh and come to the earth plane, that he might gain knowledge through experience; and most frequently his greatest wisdom is gained by making mistakes, then correcting them.

Very often young men fear to enter the marital state because harmony and happiness were lacking in the homes, or by reason of brothers or sisters unhappily mated. This is not an

excuse for avoiding the responsibility; God's great Law is—
Mate, and man's first effort should be to gain the knowledge of
what constitutes being a *man,* husband, and father; then to seek
his mate and do his best; this is his sacred duty.

Frequently we must deal with a class of men and women,
who, disappointed in a first affair of the heart, are as dead in
their emotional nature. Others, laboring under the fear of an
inherent disease do not think it best to marry. These, like the
youths, should live the continent life; *must follow the methods
outlined.* If work, exercise, recreation, transmutation, and strict
obedience to Divine Law are adhered to, health, strength and
peace may result; though honesty and experience induces us to
confess that where the youth was sullied by abuse of the creative
function, there is always the possibility of Prostatic difficulties
later in life. This is one of the penalties for disobedience to the
God-given Law commanding men to "mate and replenish the
earth," and whoso refuses to abide by the Natural and Divine
fiat is certain to pay.

The Law of Life is mating and reproduction of the specie
as a fundamental; marriage the medium for the utilization of
the creative forces and energies; for the Re-generation of the
embracing pair; ending in Immortality—the salvation of both
souls.

The Great Madness

WOMAN AND HUSBAND SHE WOULD SELL

Mrs. Lillian Russell, the Rockland, Mass., woman who would sell her husband to obtain enough money to raise their children—there are seven of them. She is 29 years of age. Friend Husband is a descendant of John Alden and a distant relative of Hetty Green. Bids open at $20.00."—*"The North American," August 27, 1920.*

Neurologists and Pyscha-Analysists are repeatedly telling us that the American people are rapidly developing into Neurotics and Neurasthenics, and if the craze for appearing in print is to be accepted as an indication, then we agree with them.

The true woman, the desirable mother, shrinks from publicity, and especially is she averse to appear in connection with any affair of the heart or motherhood.

To the worth-while mother, her family circle is sacred, and she resents any allusion to it; considering it sacrilegious to publicly refer to this relationship.

For a woman to offer her husband for sale is on a par with the action of a near-male who suggests the exploitation of his wife's body to his acquaintances—prostitution of body and soul in thought, if not in act; degrading to the self, and an accusation of Society at large.

The normal, healthy man who is unable to properly support his family should seek the appointment of a commission to examine into his responsibility; nor should a male who permits his wife to seek such notoriety resent the imputation of his fellowmen that his moral-stamina has shrunken to the pin-point dimension.

Sex Instructions in Public

Learn Wisdom from the Experience of Others

"Learn wisdom from the experience of others," indicates that it should be unnecessary for us to suffer through our own experiences when it is possible to profit by noting the acts of our fellow men, and the results naturally following them; enabling us to gain wisdom without being guilty of similar blunders.

In many departments of life we do come to a comprehension of cause and effect; but in a greater number of others, in fact, in some of the most important activities, we totally ignore the possibility, and come to an understanding only through bitter experiences.

Especially is this true in practically all that concerns the creative function. In the development of fancy cattle, prize poultry, and pedigreed dogs, not to mention swine, we employ the most noted experts to teach us the mating, housing, and feeding of the valued animals; and willingly follow their instructions that we may avoid loss, because we believe their study and experiments qualify them as instructors. But in the infinitely more important department of human life,—child culture and the development of a superior race, we not only fail to engage experts to discover for us the best food for the mother, the child, and the youth, but we refuse to listen to them when their services are offered gratis, and do *all* in our power to discourage them, bringing contempt upon all who dare to inculcate the doctrine that the sex function is the port of entrance to the development of a superior race. Often it does not end with contempt, but we condemn, shun, and occasionally, changing the usual program, by imprisoning those who through love of the unappreciative human race dare to teach mankind the truth concerning themselves and their creative potentialities.

Why is it that we are so anxious to learn all we can about animal husbandry: the mating, housing, and feeding, so attaining production of the highest grade of chickens, hogs, dogs, and cattle, while condemning those who would gladly teach us the science for the development of the human race? Is it because we really consider the sub-human creatures of greater benefit to God and the Universe? Because the Creative powers and functions of the human race are less pure than those of the animals upon whom we bestow such great care? These are issues we no longer *dare* evade.

We are more consistent in some respects; for instance, in our public schools, even in some of the lower grades, we instruct the child in the mystery of plant life,—fertilization and culture, and believe this highly desirable for its welfare; yet as a matter of fact, the creative organism of the plant is in nowise greatly different from that of the animal creative and reproductive function. We proceed along this line and in teaching horticulture, we instruct fully in the dissection of the reproductive organism of the plant, and how fertilization, both natural and artificial, takes place.

Fundamentally, *there is little difference between the creative functioning of plant, animal, and human. Why not then draw an analogy between the three departments of creation in chaste language, that child and adult can quickly comprehend the beauty, the chastity, the purity, and the necessity of sex.*

This would be the simplest, easiest, and most desirable method of teaching the child, the parent, and the public generally. The lecturer, in dealing with congregations of people, should instruct through the functional analogy of the plant which so closely resembles the human specie, and fully explain to his auditors the reproductive organism of the plant, the method of fertilization; showing clearly the similarity between plant and animal, animal and human. In this manner the mind will be able to conceive the wisdom of nature; unconscious of the morbid, destructive, and carnal thoughts and desires usually aroused when sex is the subject of a lecture, or when these problems are publicly discussed.

Is this difficult? Not in the least; text books on the culture of plants may be obtained by anyone, and through a careful study, one can readily become thoroughly conversant with the problem. Add to this animal husbandry, sex hygiene and eugenics, and one is prepared to meet the problem.

Why has this not been the approved method of procedure? Why is it not at present? Because, for so many centuries man has been taught to ignore, and abhor, the sex question and all centering around it, that the bright side of the problem has never been even thought of, much less discussed. Sex became a subject of attention only when the sun had set and the light turned out so that "darkness covered the whole face of the earth."

The first necessity, therefore, is to arrive, through careful study, at a thorough understanding of the entire subject; to learn all that may be known of the exalted and divine side of sex; then to analyze, with a clean and open mind, all that we have learned, so finding its desirable, constructive side, just as we seek, and find, the beauties in a highly developed flower.

In the consideration of this important question, we must avoid extremes; must forego to seek for the dark side of it; that which brings dishonor, disease, misery, degradation and death; though be willing to give it the recognition justified by its seriousness. We should likewise religiously avoid discussions in season and out of season; bearing in mind the Biblical injunction: "There is a time and a season for all things." We should discourage the discussion of the sex question in public gatherings of mixed audiences unless the meeting was called for that expressed purpose.

At the moment when humanity is awakening to the tremendous importance of sex hygiene, there are many opportunities for us to inculcate the truth, but we should be extremely careful to do this in a dignified manner as becomes true men and women; never making reference to anything concerning sex, in a ribald, or what might appear vulgar, manner; nor by giving our

silent consent to others who may be guilty, thereby doing grave
injury to the cause of the development of a superior race.

In attempting to discuss this great and vital subject before
the people, whether a gathering of those who desire to become
teachers; parents, or children having reached the age of comprehension of so important a subject, we must do honor to it by
our personal appearance; that it be dignified and such as to
impress upon the minds of the audience the necessity for the
truths embracing the Divine Creative Force and the glory of
race regeneration. If those to whom we bring the saving information are not fully informed, we should commence our instructions by means of analogy; thence proceed to the sub-human,
and gradually unfold the mystery of the creative power and organism of the human; illustrating, in simple language, the purpose and power of each organ of creation, designating them by
comprehensive names readily understood by the audience, yet
furtherest removed from the vulgar expressions with which every
boy and girl in school, is familiar. Therefore, our greatest success, especially before young people, depends upon our appearance and the manner in which we present the subject. If we are
thoroughly conversant with the entire problem, if we are at ease,
free from self-consciousness, and, *if we believe all that we teach,*
then it is not difficult inculcating in the young the belief that sex,
in all its offices, is both sacred and divine.

The most difficult phase is to prove to man, woman, and
youth that sex is not the degraded *office of passion* they have
always been taught, and believed, it to be; a possession heartily
to be ashamed of,—but the *highest and holiest gift from a Creative God to man.* Sex, admittedly, has a dark, a *very* dark side
to it, but this in itself is the *absolute proof of an equally bright
side.* The perversion of sex has brought disease and death to an
actually countless number; the exaltation of the same potential
force will bring health, longevity, and Immortalization. Like
all forces in nature, it is dual in its potentialities and manifestation, depending entirely upon the use, and it is left to the *free
choice* of each one of us as individuals, whether we will employ

it for glorious realization or degradatory death, and possibly destruction of the soul itself.

How many would think of using a prayer to curse another? Though there are many men who have lost all respect for religion and disclaim belief in God, yet few of these could be induced to voice a prayer for the purpose of calling down a curse upon another. Why? Because through their entire life they have been taught that prayer is for but one purpose: either to supplicate God for a favor for one's self, or calling a blessing upon another; consequently, there is but one meaning attached to prayer; and that is, for good. As a matter of fact, prayer or supplication may be as readily voiced in calling a curse upon another as in invoking a blessing; but the race has been taught only its higher use.

As with prayer, so with the procreative function. If once we can bring mankind to a realization that sex is a blessing and not a curse; a thing of beauty and not an abomination; if we can instil a comprehension that sex is like prayer, pure in itself, holy in all its natural function, and for good only, then will mankind conceive sex in a different light. Up to the present the accursed side of sex has been the only one presented to humanity, while the good has been ignored, and even denied as having existence.

Within recent years men have gone mad on business efficiency; admitting that what is usually termed "personal magnetism" is the basis of force and power underlying the mental brilliancy and alertness necessary to attain success in any line of endeavor; yet how few of these "preachers of a constructive gospel" are actually aware that this so-called "personal magnetism" is neither more nor less than a powerful sex nature; that the more fully this is developed *and controlled*, the greater the power, force, and energy; alertness and brilliancy of mind, possessed? In reality, the basis of achievement in every line of endeavor, is *virile* force; and just as the sex powers diminish, so will the creative power. In the sense we here use the word "creative power" it has reference to the capability to accomplish, to succeed, where others fail.

Like with man, so with woman. In her it manifests itself by the fire in her eyes, the freshness of her skin, the glory of her hair, the vivacity of her nature, the enchantment of her smile. We speak of her as "full of life," but few understand that all these attractive qualities are actually and fundamentally based upon a healthy sex nature, on an organism functioning normally.

Who is able to behold anything abnormal in such a man or such a woman? On the contrary, do we not speak of them as perfect, as examples whom all would do well to emulate; but not for one moment do we associate their personality with the healthfulness and naturalness of the creative functions; though as an uncontradictable fact, all that is desirable in their entire being is based absolutely on the creative potency, naturally, normally, healthily, and fully developed.

Having the knowledge of these principles we do, it is our sacred duty to teach the truth to every unit of every audience before whom we appear; and prove to them to the full extent of our ability, that while it is on a normal, healthy, and fully developed sex nature these desirable qualities in man are based, it must not be abused, else the penalty is fearful to contemplate. If we can induce men and women, fathers and mothers, boys and girls, to comprehend this great truth, and show them it is the foundation of a true life, *that exalted sex is the power of attraction,* then we have removed from the mind that dark and sinister side held before it for many centuries.

Those who have abused the creative privileges granted them by their Creator, look upon the function with shame; these are the individuals who are always loudest in their denunciation of all instructions concerning sex. "To the pure in heart all things are pure," but these have misused their sacred privileges and the "veil of purity" has fallen from their eyes. Like Paul before his conversion, they see "as with eyes darkly."

The individual who employs his creative functions for ignoble purposes poisons the Fountain of Life, and creates a diseased mind, a perverted imagination, and a darkening aspect of the subject. The misuse brings shame; clearly illustrated in the Biblical allegory of the Garden of Eden episode. While Eve loved the natural life, she saw nothing impure, or to be ashamed of, in her nudity. To both her and to her partner Adam, their bodies were pure, holy, created by God in the highest art; but the moment they abused their creative nature,—by indulgence for the satisfaction of passion, without a desire for generation or regeneration; and with the effort to *prevent the natural consequence of the act,—* their minds became assailed with a sense of shame and their nudity became as a "nakedness which had to be concealed."

In this one story illustrating the result following the abuse of the creative power, we can find material for a thousand sermons; it proves conclusively that it is not the pure in heart and clean in mind who condemn true sex science, but such as those who, through immoral relations have discovered their own nakedness. In their own light they see all others; naked and defiled in the sight of God their Creator who, in calling them forth, saw that "all was good." How will these answer their God when He demands of them: "What hast thou done with the talents I gave thee?"

Sex is like a good medicine, which, when rightly employed induces health; but wrongly used produces disease, misery, and death. The creative function is in itself pure and holy, and correctly utilized is a means of generation as well as for Regeneration—a rebuilding of the entire being; when abused it is like poison to the mental faculties; it colors the imagination darkly, induces morbidy, clouds the imaginative faculty of the mind, brings sorrow and misery, ends in death, if not in total extinction. It is not the power that is to be condemned, but the vile and carnal mis-use men make of it.

The potency of this force for either good or evil is readily illustrated: Take for example a young man living a natural life, one full of virility and vital force, call it personal magnetism, if you will. He readily attracts people; he easily retains his friends, and accomplishes that which to others seems impossible. As a fact, he quickly passes hundreds on the way who are apparently much more talented than he; all this he does simply, naturally, and unconsciously; it seems as though the gods and fates were continually smiling upon him.   Through some unwise association he contracts habits destructive to his well-being; he commences the misuse of the creative functions; he drains his vitality through pleasurable exercises; gradually the fire fades from his eyes; his attractiveness leaves him; his friends feel he has changed; he is no longer magnetic.   The work formerly accomplished with ease becomes labor; his appearance of youth gives place to that of age.   Why this great change?   Because he has degraded his inheritance, depleted the "storage batteries" below normal, and is beginning to reap the results of disobedience.

This is one of the most emphatic lessons indicating the desirability of a powerfully developed sex nature, and a knowledge of the correct use for creative *and* re-creative purposes only, *never* for the satisfaction of desire; passion is ignoble; induces weakness and disease, finally ending in death.

The Great Madness

Women's Dress and Men's Morality

"The way the girls dress is appalling and invites men to follow them."

"Men have no respect for women and women seem to glory in the fact."

From the state of a real Russian princess to that of a waitress in Child's, from the splendors of palaces to the squalor of New York's lower East Eide; from a royal lady, commanding homage, to a shop girl in a department store—to these ends did the princess go to investigate moral conditions in New York City.

"Where else than in America," Princess Radziwill asks, "do we see women powdering and rouging and dressing their hair in public? The way the girls dress is appalling, and invites men to follow them, to put it mildly. When a man sees a woman in a street car with nothing beneath a thin dress but a satin slip, its hooks not even fastened, not even the thinnest of undergarments, what can he think and what can he expect?

"Watch only at the door of one of our large stores at the hour when its employees leave in the evening. Watch girls go lightly to an appointed place, jump into the luxury of a waiting limousine in which its owner usually sits, and be spirited away to some spot unfrequented by his friends for dinner."—*The North American, Philadelphia, September 13, 1920.*

Because a certain class of men, admittedly a very large one, applaud the immorality in dress and behavior, and the indiscretions of deluded girls and women, is not indicative that these men have respect for such foolish and silly enough to be led astray by flatteries and a surfeit of luxury clandestinely presented. On the contrary, even the semi-libertine when seeking a wife, does not in the least favor one of the painted, powdered, short-skirted, low-waisted, and almost nude girls who so freely exchange all most sacred for "a good time." While the men who really respect womanhood and motherhood, who still retain an ideal in the heart, made sacred by the goodness, purity, and chastity of their own mothers, would not even associate with these, much less think of marrying them. Do men admire the nude or semi-nude form of woman? Undoubtedly so, but they have no respect for any woman foolish enough to display such in public; and when seeking a woman to love and cherish they are *extremely jealous that no other man shall have looked upon that beloved form; to them alone belongs the right to lift the veil.*

Preparing for the Baby

"That which is worth doing is worth doing well."

Practically all of us are familiar with this old precept; though few of us are governed by it in all our actions. A maxim directly applicable to the important subject under consideration would be: "If a child is to be born it has a right to be born well."

God's greatest and most sublimely mysterious gift to man is the power of Procreation; yet very few of the teeming millions ever give it so much as a thought; undoubtedly due to the fact that creation of the human specie is almost always an accident, rather than a carefully planned performance of a Sacred duty. So far Nature has had the entire responsibility placed upon her by an ignorant and prejudiced humanity. Now that the Laws of Heredity and Pre-natal influence are studied and taught, let us hope She will be relieved of at least part of the task.

The law of Heredity deals with the inheritance of the good, and less-good, qualities native to the parents, and which possibly were transmitted to them by grandparents, or even great-grand-parents. The law of Pre-natal influences govern the impressions upon the child, of qualities, powers, and virtues possibly lacking in both parents, but which they desire the child to possess. It will be readily understood that Pre-natal influences are of far greater importance than the Law of Heredity; the Pre-natal influences having the potential power to either modify, or entirely set aside, Heredity.

Irrespective of the fact that many scientific men ridicule the possibility of investing the unborn with powers and virtues not possessed by the parents, we maintain that the mother can, by surrounding herself with works of art, beautiful paintings, and objects which elevate the thoughts, and by gazing upon them often, meanwhile concentrating her desires on impressing the child in her bosom with loftiness of mind, strength and beauty of physique, and greatness of soul, give birth to a superior being.

Though scientists smile at the simplicity of minds having faith in the power of such impressions on the unborn, for good, we seriously question whether they would allow us to display at the foot of the bed wherein sleep their wives when *en ceinte*, pictures depicting fearful accidents, the carnage of war, or of men with misshapen bodies or ugly countenances. We feel certain they would not; they would inform us that such pictures were potent to affect mind and nerves of the mothers, and indirectly the well-being of the unborn.

This assertion we would at once admit, though we are forced to question in all sincerity on what reason they base their claim that pictures depicting undesirable scenes and misshapen personalities have the power to influence conscious and unconscious minds, while they deny the power of the beautiful and aesthetic to impress the mother-to-be and child, for good. Is not *every* law dual? Must not the negative have a positive? Is there not a magnetic force for every electric, and a North pole for every South? The Laws governing the incentives and actions of Life are also dual, not single and unbalanced.

One of the most simple and authoritative accounts of prenatal influence or maternal impressions, is given in the Biblical account of Jacob and the sheep. In this it is clearly indicated that even the animal nature is sufficiently impressable so that colors and types may be produced almost at will. If the truths of these Biblical narratives are admitted, is anyone, scientist or philosopher, hardy enough to claim that the nature of woman, whose nervous system is the finest and most delicate of all creation, less impressionable and responsive to the beautiful than the animal? *Au contrari*, if scientist and philosopher deny the Biblical record, then they must likewise question every other statement in the Bible.

In the present scientific age we give every attention to the breeding of animals; we carefully study their characteristics and their vims; we seek to know what they like or dislike; we give attention to the question of food; withholding from them those they do not like, and supplying them with such they prefer. When we mate them we are most careful in the selection of the sire, and we remove everything from their presence which seems to in the least irritate them. We *know from experience* that all these things have a powerful influence on both the mature animal and the unborn.

How has it been in the great, mysterious, sublime realm of human creation? Have we given study as to the best time when conception should take place? Have we taught humanity the right season for the propagation of the Specie? Have we made a study of the proper preparation for the conceiving mother? Have we taught womanhood generally when this period occurs? Have we studied the great problem of proper diet, and have we taught people generally the sane conclusions reached? Have we studied the impressions of the beautiful on her mental and nervous systems during this trying time? Have we watched the effects of the ugly and undesirable, and taught her how to avoid, or that failing, to overcome these depressing influences? Have we taught the feminine world the serious consequences of reading exciting and morbid literature? Have we been patient in our research and willingly offered to all the fruits of our labors, or have we allowed the entire affair to take care of itself, ignorance to be as potent in the weakening and degradation of the race as in the time of our forefathers, still trusting to Nature to produce a god, while supplying her with the material and opportunity unsuited to the creation of even an idiot.

Men and women have not as yet awakened to even a partial comprehension of the potentialities with which Nature has endowed them; they have not become conscious of their great responsibility, duties and possibilities in the creative sphere. Thus far every thought has been of themselves, their own salvation; the idea never entering their mind that not alone are they burdened by God's great law with their own welfare, but likewise accountable for that of their children, their children's children, and even their great-grandchildren.

Mothers and fathers must quickly awaken to their *rights* as also their *responsibilities*. There is a sinister movement rapidly taking form, the intentions of which are undoubtedly commendable; but it is leading the race towards the

SHOALS AHEAD

We have reference to the activity of men and women, for the most part composed of women who have never been mothers; having not the slightest idea of what the feeling of motherhood would be; and of men who have thus far refused to accept the responsibility of fatherhood. Their idea is the formation of a department of public welfare, the enactment of laws governing the instruction and training of the children. So far well, but the ulterior object is to take from the *bona fide* mothers and fathers throughout the land, *the control and training, the intellectual, and even the spiritual direction of the children.* In Sparta of old this was actually accomplished—*that nation is now known only in name.* In foreign countries such efforts are more or less successful, but we foresee that when this is actually attempted in America, the entire *motherhood will arise in their might as one, the governing power sanctioning it will be swept aside as a straw in the wind, and the deluded men and women who select themselves to wrest a child from its rightful mother, will thereby seal their own doom.*

God's greatest blessing, as also His greatest privilege, is sacred motherhood. It is our duty to study the problem and teach mothers and mothers-to-be, but no loving man or woman, shirking the responsibility of fatherhood or motherhood, has any moral or spiritual right to come between the family.

The problem of Heredity must have our careful consideration. We must instruct both men and women in its influence on the unborn. This we can best do by concrete examples.

In 1909 the Physio-Medical Society of the State of Indiana held its convention at Indianapolis; and during one of the sessions, a carefully prepared paper dealing with the problem of Heredity, was read by one of the members of the Society.

It appeared there lived in the Western part of Pennsylvania, a family then little known but later to become extremely notorious. To this family was born a girl, more or less mentally weak and as usual at the time, even as at the present, with the exception of feeding and clothing her, she had little attention, no instruction or training, and no one to see that no evil befell her.

This girl, ignorant, unprepared, and unprotected, was betrayed by a male brute with the usual result; a female child was born to her. The parents, instead of doing their duty and exercising every effort in their power that neither she nor her child should become the victims of other such renegades, cast both of them on society. Neither society nor State had the slightest inclination to look after the outcasts, with the result that they were the beginning of a long line of degenerate men and women. The record, as given, was this:

"Sixty members of the descendants had court records, fifteen had been in jail, fourteen in the penitentiary, nine in the infirmary, nine in children's homes, six in the workhouse, two in the Girls' Industrial Home, two in the Institution for Feeble-minded, and one in the Boys' Industrial Home.

"Seventy-seven were immoral, seventy-four criminal in varying degrees, fifty-five feeble-minded, twenty-three alcoholic, twelve public women, seven tubercular, six children adopted into homes, four epileptics, three insane, and three wanderers who labored not.

"Among the crimes of which some of these were guilty, we find catalogued burglary, forgery, destruction of property, owning or inmates of immoral houses, intoxication, rioting, perjury, various degenerating practices, homicide, and poisoning with intent to kill.

"The mentality of the degenerate members of the family was that of children between seven and twelve years."

To whom does condemnation belong? Is the poor victim, through whom this long line of degenerates had its beginning, alone to bear the penalty? We maintain she was least to blame; *she was wrongly born; ignorant, receiving neither training nor warning, such as was hers by right of having been thrust into a cold world. She was uninstructed in the ways of life; nor so enlightened as to avoid becoming a mother; or conceiving, possessing the knowledge to impregnate her progeny with strength of mind and body such as she did not possess.*

Undoubtedly the foregoing is a fearful picture to behold, it is nevertheless merely illustrative of other instances of like nature; and though we practically exempt this woman from blame, knowing her weakness and ignorance, we cannot do as much for the modern woman, because she has every opportunity to gain knowledge of the laws governing the creative functions; laws which will free her from the bondage so long shackling her sex.

It is possible for any woman of ordinary intelligence to become the mother of a race of mental giants, physical gods, and moral and spiritual masters. How? By teaching her all those duties which she owes to herself as a woman; to think constructively; read good books; selecting foods for their building and cleansing value; exercises to develop her entire physical being, and all the laws governing the "building" of a new creature of the specie.

She loves, she marries, she conceives; she personally selects books whose contents will have good influences on the mind of both herself and the coming child, be it boy or girl. She allows neither obscene nor shocking pictures in the house and is especially careful in the selection of those for her own chamber. She associates only with cultured people who use chaste language; she attends plays that are refining and constructive. She is careful of bathing; indulges in cold baths in the morning, internal baths when necessary. Faithfully follows a system of physical exercises and breathing drills; keeps fully and interestingly occupied, and avoids everything that might possibly be nerve shocking or induce hysteria. Above all, she is careful in the selection of her diet, avoiding all articles of food that could possibly congest the system and interfere with good circulation and resultant clear brain.

She refuses sexual relationship with her husband unless first brought to a keen desire by his caresses; is sufficiently mentally unshackled, and mother enough to indicate her real feelings when her wedded partner fails to notice them. Let a woman thus trained, living such a life, conceive, impress, and give birth to a child, and it will be the beginning of a regenerate Race.

Let us suppose this child is a girl; the mother instructs her in the truth as she was taught; trains her under all the laws governing the development of her own womanhood; this child reaching adolescence, then motherhood, in her turn teaches and develops her children in like manner, can we even begin to estimate what this will mean to the nation within a few generations? We can, however, form an opinion of the influence such superior men and women would have on the affairs of nations, their morals being uncorruptible.

It cannot be successfully argued that this is an idle dream; of an ideal state; impractical in every day life. Men and women *can* as readily obtain good literature as destructive, vulgar, and obscene publications. They have no greater difficulty in securing beautiful pictures than those depicting destruction or vulgarity. They can keep mind and body occupied instead of catering to their "nerves"; can walk and exercise in place of lounging about the house or club; and have the choice of attending good plays and operas instead of choosing questionable shows; above all, they can obtain good, nutritious, nerve and brain building foods as cheaply as rich meats, sweets, cookies, candies, spiced articles, and useless desserts having no actual value to the body, but clogging the entire eliminative system, and producing weakness and low mental states.

The true life is no more difficult to live than is a destructive existence; it is merely a question of choice. Many are perfectly satisfied to live in an old, leaky hovel, though they had the opportunity to move into a modern, sanitary, well-appointed dwelling; likewise, the majority prefer the old, irresponsible, destructive, negative life. The creative life requires no self denial, merely the desire to do the right thing in the right place and at the right time; it forbids no innocent pleasure, no harmless recreation, no good food, nor any enjoyment that gives happiness.

Man boasts of being the lord of creation, but consider his consistency for a moment.

The farmer who masters his vocation, studies the requirements of his soil, supplies it with its deficiencies, plows and carefully prepares his fields. When the time arrives to sow, he patronizes a dealer in seeds in whom he has confidence and selects only the choicest, those having been tested for germination. He gives strict attention to the proper time for the sowing; choosing days he believes will be best for the purpose, always having in mind the germination of the seeds. After the seed has been planted, every care and constant cultivation is given it, assuring a crop equalling his expectation, and if possible, showing improvement over the seed sown. And all for what? That he may be supplied with food for the Winter, or for conversion into money wherewith to secure pleasures or necessities of life.

Now consider the propagators of the greatest of all crops —the human family. How many labor to know the Law governing the function, that the place of sowing may be prepared; that the seed may be strong, healthy and vital? How many watch for the right time to sow; and are vigilant while the seed is forming a new being? How many continue their watchfulness after the seed has manifested, and continue faithfully until it is grown.

Very few indeed! To the many procreation is of no importance. Nature can look after her own labors. Moreover, most frequently he would rather the seed did not germinate and take root, as a fact, many times he does all in his power to prevent it from even reaching the fertile soil. If, despite his every effort, children are born with an inheritance of weakness, with criminal tendencies, always ill, a source of sorrow, does he not roundly curse God for visiting upon him—the lord of creation—that which he, in his criminal ignorance and arrogance, called into being?

If we desire strong, healthy, superior babies, we must go back a step beyond consideration of the Laws of Heredity and Pre-natal influences; beginning with the children already born, carefully instructing them in all the Laws of Procreation; preparing them for the great work before them; and through training eradicate all that is weak and undesirable, before they have even reached the age of responsibility.

We should teach them in all the Laws pertaining to Environments, Imitation, Personal and Pre-natal Influence, and Heredity; that they may employ all of the knowledge when they become Co-creators with God. We must impress upon them the necessity of thorough preparation; that thus is half the battle won; that while Heredity is the foundation, and Pre-natal influences and impressions are the building, one is equally as important as the other.

Is this labor worth the effort? Seemingly, while we are in youth and the world looks bright and rosy to us, and we have no little ones of our own whose suffering we must witness, it is not; but as we advance in years, as many little feet cross our path, some of them our own, as we see their suffering and are helpless to relieve it, we begin to appreciate the vast importance of doing our best to either prevent, or at least to partially minimize this misery and sorrow, rather than merely seeking a remedy to temporarily relieve it.

The fearful price we, as a nation, pay for the heedless and senseless fashion in which our children are conceived, born and reared, is readily comprehended when we understand that in the United States alone there are more than one million weaklings and degenerates filling our prisons and insane asylums; though in this vast multitude we do not include the almost numberless army suffering from advanced stages of syphilis, cancer, tuberculosis and various other filthy blood diseases, generally directly caused by depravities of nature.

In no department of creation or reproduction is man as neglectful and ignorant as in that of the birth and development of his children; and he wilfully avoids the subject as though it did not in the least concern him. while the awful penalty he pays in misery and suffering seems impotent to awaken him to the light of day.

Truly "none are so blind as those who will not see."

The Great Madness

Rabbi Krauskopf Fears U. S. Tends to Decadence

"The indecent dress adopted by women of all classes, the vulgar dances, the immoral plays, the ease and frequency with which divorces are obtained, and the many other forms of moral depravity practiced in America, are one day, unless they are curbed in time, going to humble this great country and make it the slave of its enemies. Repentance will come, and lament will come, but repentance and lament will come too late.

"Whenever and wherever a people substitute the worship of gold for that of God and make indulgence of animal lusts its ruling passion, its decadence has set in and its day of ruin is not far distant.

"Every day we hear of goings-on that cannot but make the true lover of this country tremble for its future. Think of the styles of dress that, at one time, constituted the costumes of women who were rigidly excluded from decent society. * * * Today these styles are adopted unblushingly by women who believe themselves to be the very cream of society.

"Think of the questionable places which young women cf good households are permitted to frequent unchaperoned and far into the night. Think of the general disregard of parental authority, of the loss of reverence for age and respect for learning.—*Rabbi Krauskopf, The North American, September 14, 1920.*

Who is to blame? Let the Rabbi question his own soul.

Do not the established churches silently give their approval by allowing all these transgressors to remain members of the church and *receive communion, the unvoiced forgiveness of their iniquities?* Does he know of any influential member of the church who has been "read out of it" for profiteering; ungentlemanly conduct; attending immoral shows, or doing any of those things condemned by those chaste of thought?

In condemning divorces and attempting to force two people to live together as man and wife, who do not love each other, cohabiting and propagating unwanted children, is not the church encouraging prostitution, legalized, to be sure, but prostitution nevertheless, and are not such children. conceived and born in lust and aversion, candidates for a life of evil?

To help save the race, the church must quickly "face about" and seek causes, find them, then quickly combat them, irrespective of the power or the standing, of the guilty.

The Law of Transmission

Heredity

No one is in a better position to prove and exemplify the Law of Transmission, usually termed Heredity, than the breeder of pedigreed stock. With him there is no chance, every animal is marked, and no opportunity afforded them to mate unknowingly. When he mates Gypsy of Beverly to Bonita the Third, he has detailed information before him of both the weak and strong points possessed by them; he has a right to expect certain characteristics in the young of the pair; if these are missing, if weakness or underdevelopment is present, he must seek for the cause either in the care of the female during the period of gestation, or a "throw-back" of several generations.

In the law of transmission in its influence on the human specie, heredity undoubtedly governs, but so many factors enter that the Law itself hardly ever has the chance of working out naturally; being modified or intensified by the mental influence of the parents, especially that of the mother, more certainly than by any other force.

In animal husbandry, this influence does not at all enter, because animals have no "mental attitude." They obey only the natural law; mating in the right season if given their choice. If the breeder selects the time for the service, and it is either too late or too previous, there will be no results. After the female conceives, the male never seeks cohabitation thereafter.

Mating and the bearing of young in the animal kingdom is in obedience of natural law; the owner merely selecting mates suited to each other.

We learn best by illustration. For more than ten years we have experimented in the breeding of fancy poultry, and five years have been devoted to raising pedigreed Collies.

For a female short in head and weak in coat, we select for service a male lengthy of head and with heavy coat. By so doing we expect the male to transmit to the young his heaviness of coat as well as length of head. However, admittedly, we are confronted with the *great unknown*: Which of the mating pair *possesses the greater vitality?* If the female is stronger than the male then it is altogether possible for her to transmit to the young her own characteristics; the head of her young being much like her own, while even despite the potency of her greater vitality, we still expect heavier coats for the young than she possesses, because vital force is one of the factors of a heavy coat. If the male possesses the greater strength, then we certainly look forward to puppies with long heads; but even here an unknown law often governs, some characteristics of a former generation may manifest.

This law can be even more clearly illustrated. We have several distinct types of Collies. The one mostly known is the Sable and White; next the Tricolor, usually known as black and white—being black of body, white markings and a sable round the eyes and possibly mouth; then the Blue Merle.

By mating a pair of Sable and White we would naturally look for young of the same color, though the tint may be modified more or less. But there is no certainty; it is altogether possible that out of a litter of six healthy pups, five will be Sable and White, while the sixth may be a Tricolor. What is the reason for such an occurence? It merely indicates that several generations back, one of the ancestors, either of the male or female, was a Tricolor, and that in the blood of one of the present parents there still remain some of the blood cells of this foreparent which impregnated. Thus a "throw-back" or reversion of type. This impregnation of a cell of a former generation is identical to the transmission from parent to child of a disease, such as syphilis, though the transmitter is apparently not in the least afflicted with it. Of this we will speak later.

If a pair of fairly evenly matched Collies are mated, let us say of desired length of head, heaviness of coat, and strength of bone; *not too closely related;* if the care and the food of the female is as it should be, we may confidently expect the young to possess the features of the parents; healthy and strong, and of like color.

Such a rule does not govern the human family. If the parents are too much alike in features, temperaments and other characteristics, even though not at all related, the children resulting from the union, if any, may be the direct opposite of the parents, possibly even be weaklings, if not perverts.

In the human family, the rule generally governing is; "Like produces like;" the vitality of the parents being equal, the likeness is more frequently after the mother than the father; due to the fact that while the father supplies the seed of life, and all of the future human monad is contained in this Spermatzoo, including the basis for health or the inoculation of an inherited disease, as the case may be, it is the mother who fashions the new being through her mental attitude during the period of gestation. The thoughts of her mind, the passions of her entire being, and the emotions of the heart, profoundly impressing the being in the process of creation.

If the mother-to-be is fully enlightened in the Creative law, she is enabled to bring forth a God-man, a Superior Being, even though the father is practically a non-entity; and her work can even extend to giving the child a healthy body, and powerful virility though the father is a weakling, provided, of course, his blood is not filled with germs of syphilis or cancer, and his nerves and brain untainted with insanity. We modify this last statement and claim that even these—cancer and syphilis—can be eliminated by the mother during the time of gestation.

Although we have made the statement that most frequently the child favored the mother; we do not wish to be understood as maintaining that this is always so. A superior man wedded to an honest, lovable, but inferior woman, is enabled to father a genius by obedience to the law following.

The period wherein man possesses the greatest creative potency is while he desires most the marital embrace and is filled with love. It is at such moments that he corrals every force within his being, and if the Marriage Rite is consummated at this time, at the moment of the climax he is positive in every faculty of his little world. If the woman granted his request after thoroughly awakening to desire through endearments, giving him her love; if he, during the entire embrace, especially at the moment of highest bliss, concentrates his mind on the one object of calling into existence a healthy, normal, and superior child, *he is enabled to draw the potential forces from heaven itself*, and this longing, hurled into space, will be granted. He is enabled to still further influence the health, strength and character of the coming child by at each embrace concentrating all his energies for these purposes, thereby charging the vital fluids given to and absorbed by the mother-to-be; so helping her to build body, nerve and brain in the new creation

If both man and woman understand the secrets of Race Regeneration, the propagation of healthy, normal, natural and God-like offspring is much less complicated; and we venture to say that ten wedded couples who truly love and have full comprehension of the law, faithfully practicing its tenets, could completely revolutionize this old world; their progeny would be so positive, virile and influential, as to enable them to rule the races with beneficence.

While the mother's influence is naturally much greater in fashioning the character and features of the child, than is the father's, she cannot readily inoculate it with such a disease as syphilis. When diseases are transmitted by the father it is through the life germ in the seminal fluid; though when this does occur it is not always an indication that he is diseased, because it is entirely possible that his father, or grandfather, or even great grandfather, may have been the sufferer and that the germs transmitted from generation to generation have been dormant up to the time they became part of the new creation.

While various diseases are usually inherited from the father, mental conditions, especially insanity and neurotic tendencies, are most frequently impressed or absorbed from the mother; every condition of her mind having an influence upon that of the unborn; it therefore behooves her to be extremely careful of her mental attitude while *en ceinte.*

When we leave the boundary of the physical and enter the realms of the purely mental, we meet with apparently serious contradictions relative to the Law of Heredity. For instance, it is generally known that most of the sons of great men are seldom an honor; while those of financial giants are hardly ever successful. At a first superficial glance this would indicate a contradiction of the law, actually it is not.

A man may once have been a physical giant and while the possessor of such strength could undoubtedly have fathered an equally potent progeny. Gradually, through abuse or negligence he deteriorates into a weakling, yet remaining capable of procreation; his offspring at this period would hardly be comparable to those resulting in his former virile condition. For an almost similar reason the great philosopher, victorious general, or powerful magnate, seldom becomes the father of sons and daughters comparable to him, *because his whole mind and all his energies are utilized in the special labor he is engaged, and there remains little strength or potency for procreation.* As a fact, he may be hardly aware of his indulgence, embracing his partner possibly because he considers it his duty; at her instigation; or at the urge of a temporary sensual desire; *very seldom, if ever,* because he longs to call into being one like unto himself. Procreation with him is entirely an accident, one for which both he and his progeny suffer deeply. Were he to set aside his vocation or avocation for a time, husband all his forces and energies, both mental and physical, and then concentrate them all in one holy act of creation, the world would be astounded at the result, while he and the Great Creator would be glorified.

Another reason children most frequently favor the mother, all other things being equal, is, that while procreation is a passing fancy or an accident on the part of the father, it absorbs all life of the mother; her energies, thoughts and desires are concentrated on the task before her; consequently she continually impressed her personality, with its likes and dislikes, upon the creation within her bosom.

Although Heredity undoubtedly underlies our strength as our weakness, it should not be the excuse for any undesirable inheritance we possess. Any one not physically or mentally all he should be, or would like to be, should not place the blame on being thus born. The inheritance of a weak body does not give man the slightest excuse for remaining so during all of a lifetime; experience daily indicating that many of the really great statesman, athletes, and philosophers, as others who have won world renown, were not born with any great physical strength, mental power, or financial backing, but obtained all of them through a refusal to bow the knee to fate, and personal effort on their part, resulting in overcoming every obstacle and undesirable quality.

Similarly, because a man inherits syphilis from, or through, one of his parents, is no legitimate excuse for him to be a victim of this filthy, degrading and destructive disease through his entire life and to die from it while still in youth. He is enabled through force of will, cleanliness and saneness of life, to eradicate it from his system; becoming as undefiled as if neither his parents or he himself had ever been contaminated with it.

We should fully recognize the Law of Transmission; but it is likewise our indisputable duty to seek understanding of the greater Law: *That we are what we make of ourselves.* That we are a combination of how we live, the food we eat, the thoughts we think, the desires we harbor, and our efforts to overcome or succeed. It unquestionably requires a powerful mental effort on the part of those born weak to gain strength and then begin a life potential for accomplishment. The Law of Heredity should not greatly concern those already born; these should search themselves and find their weakness or impotency, then overcome it. We should seriously consider the Law of Transmission as it concerns the unborn, and feel it our duty to enlighten the world of its power to influence the physical, mental and spiritual welfare of those yet to be born, that these may not be burdened with the weaknesses and vices now cursing the multitudes.

Humanity should be shown its duty, not to attempt calling a new creature into being unless it is really wanted and they themselves are mentally and physically strong at the moment. That just as they would carefully prepare the foundation for a house they proposed building, so is it essential to their own welfare, as well as that of society at large, to likewise prepare the substructure for the prototype of themselves they are about to call into existence. Having given their attention to this first preparation, the next step is to choose the proper time; as when they are at their best physically, mentally and morally; seeking not merely the pleasures of the embrace, but the fruits thereof as well.

When conception has occurred, the parents have definite duties to perform. The husband should give strict attention respecting his treatment of his wife; never causing her annoyance in any way as to her person; nor approach her unless he has reason to assume his presence be desirable.

The embrace may be undertaken only in its highest aspect; love and affection, not passion, is to be the incentive, nor may it be discontinued until her conjugal love is fully requitted. Moreover, the rite must never be undertaken unless *she* actually desires *it*, and no more frequently than required by her for her well-being, lest a longing be impressed upon the unborn. Equally important to understand that if the mother-to-be courts the embrace and is refused, the child may be born love hungry, a Magdalene, through no fault of its own.

These are a few of the important considerations in the procreation of a new entity; though admittedly under present conditions the average husband has no understanding of the Law; is governed by his desires; disgusts his mate by inconsiderate attentions; and thus forever impresses the child with like aversion; damning it through all the days of its life; creating in its nature desires ending in perversions, or cold and devoid of feeling. On the contrary, if the father labors under the erroneous impression that it is wrong to have sexual congress with the mother while *en ceinte,* and she suffers from love hunger during this period, the child is almost certain to be impressed with this craving all its life, manifesting it by being unhappy in the companionship of one man or one woman; forever seeking, but never satisfied.

The mother-to-be has equally a duty to the unborn. She must govern her mental attitude so as not to impress the child with impatience, hysteria, or the many other emotions resultant of an unsettled mind. She must build up the body through proper food, bathing and exercises, elevating her mental forces by right thinking, cheerfulness, chaste thoughts, and the reading of good books, listening to good music, and the indulgence in healthful and wholesome recreations. The mother's duties are tremendous; if she fulfills them she will be compensated a thousand-fold; the love she harbors in her heart and mind for the unborn will be the connecting link binding the child to her and to God in the years before her.

Many women develop a strange and apparently unreasonable appetite during the period of gestation. If this is for something which is in itself harmful, it must be refused. If it is not harmful, then it should be supplied as quickly as possible, thus avoiding making an undesirable impression on the unborn.

Irrespective of her opinions on morality, the mother-to-be should read no literature which savors of loose morality, and under no circumstances permit any conversation in her hearing which is not chaste. She should not associate with indi viduals of questionable character; at the same time make every effort to elevate her thoughts, desires and inclinations for all that she feels angels would choose; no habit, weakness or quality is as easily transmitted as a weak moral nature; such an inheritance being the incentive to become a white slaver, a Magdalene of the street, libertine, debauchee, or pervert.

Every passion, appetite, desire, emotion and weakness is readily transmittable to the child during gestation. *This is the Law.*

The Great Madness

Charges Suffrage Coarsens Women

"Knoxville, Tenn., July 7.—Miss Annie Bock, of Los Angeles, formerly an equal suffrage leader, in a letter to W. K. Anderson, representative in the lower house of the Tennessee Legislature and a candidate for another term, urges him not to support ratification of the suffrage amendment. * * *

"I was one of the prominent workers who helped to bring suffrage to California, and I regret it.

"A year in politics has taught me that women are intolerant, radical, revolutionary and more corrupt in politics than men, also all this so-called reform leads to the Socialist co-operation commonwealth.

"Since suffrage there has been alarming increase in immorality, divorce and murder in California.

"Woman suffrage has made cowards and puppets of men. It has coarsened and cheapened women.

"Suffragists asked suffrage that they might put only good men in office; now they clamor for a fifty-fifty show for all offices."

Miss Bock is as radical and irrational as Mrs. Catt. Suffrage has *not* coarsened women, *it has merely offered a vehicle for a certain class of women through which to manifest the nature of the male which formerly could not suitably express itself.*

Suffrage has *not* changed the real woman, the true mother. She shrinks from publicity; she does not enter politics; does not mix in the affairs of men. When she does vote, it is done quietly; without display of a homo-sexuality. She is a woman, God's ward.

Suffrage has *not* made men either cowards or puppets. Cowards and puppets are born, not made. Women in politics have simply offered these weaklings an opportunity to display the vulgar side of feminity.

Marriage

The Wedding Night

"He Who Begins With His Wife With Rape Is Lost."—*Arabian*

Unquestionably the great majority of men do just this on their wedding night and are never again able to command the respect and love their wives had for them as their lovers.

Woman has been peculiarly constituted by the Creator. It is immaterial how deeply she may love, and how great her longing to be possessed, or how ready and willing to give herself to the embrace, she nevertheless expects her suitor to entreat her for the favor requested; and *confidently hopes he will caress her into submission.* This is born in the heart of every *real, womanly* woman; and all men would do well to study this phase of her nature. If he is truly a man, if he but partially understands her, he will play his part with knightly bearing, feeling within himself that she has a right to expect this much from him and that if the desire is worth suing for, compliance with the longing of her nature will be greatly repaid.

The misery and unhappiness rampant in the lives of most married people had its inception through actions resultant of ignorance. The man receives no instructions relative his actions and duties, rights and privileges. He has in mind but one idea; the privileges he believes belong to him; is totally unaware of the duties evolving on him with the acceptance of the favors he expects. He imagines that his whole duty is fulfilled when he gains her consent to become his wife, marrying her, providing a home, and supplying her with the necessary clothing and food. In exchange for this he believes she is bound to take care of the home, grant his requests when he is minded to make them, and bear his children when they accidently result. Often she is just as much at fault, expecting a home; possessions making life desirable; very little self-denial and sorrows, with much love which she imagines should be as nearly sexless as possible.

Laboring under such false conceptions relative to their duties and privileges, the average couple are wed; enter the marriage chamber; and emerge therefrom in the morning, very much the wiser, though a great deal sadder, for their experience of a few short hours; with disgust and a cooling love for him on her side, and dissatisfaction with her on his side. As an illustration, let us cite a case of which we happen to possess all the facts.

The young man we have in mind looked upon woman as the queen of heaven; would not believe that any could stoop to sell her body; and had an idea that all of them were very much misunderstood—in which last supposition he was undoubtedly more or less correct. This youngster had some knowledge of sex laws, though totally ignorant in the wisdom making man a successful lover. He "fell in love" with a young lady of nearly his own age and believing his emotion fully reciprocated, married her.

They entered the bridal chamber, and like all of his kind—naturally so—he requested, sued and coaxed for the privilege of a complete consummation of the marriage rite. Do what he would, the lady refused, turned away from him, and rather coldly informed him that had she married a young man of her acquaintance (a former suitor), she felt that he would have loved her without making such a request.

The young man's ideals relative to women, love, marriage and the inception and birth of children were extremely high; and he would never have given a thought to marriage unless he believed in the love of the woman; one can therefore readily picture the effect such a statement had upon him. It chilled him to the very center of his soul, and the love he formerly had for the woman who was now his wife suffered a shock from which it never fully recovered; ever after, the memory of the incident remained to loom up ghost-like when he decided to repeat his request.

This experience is merely an example of countless others, with slight modifications one way or another, daily occurring throughout the world. In the main it is a direct result of the faulty instructions girls receive from their mothers. Many of these mothers are frigid by nature, having been begotten by mothers cold and embittered in heart, who were ignorant enough to instruct their daughters in the delusion that there can be love between man and woman not based on sex or its gratification. This is the most dangerous misunderstanding under which a girl can labor; it is wholly devoid of truth and destructive to her happiness if she attempts to govern her actions harmoniously with it.

The girl should be minutely instructed in both her duties and her rights before she enters the bonds of wedlock. She must be clearly informed that passion is not love; that it can exist without a basis in love, and when satisfied there is no longer any desire for the companionship of the one who was its victim. But, what is of greater importance to her happiness, she must be taught that while there is love without passion among the angels, and a semblance of the divine emotion in the weakly and impotent, there can be no such ecstacy in the hearts of real men and women without passion; because Nature has seen fit to base conjugal love in companionship with passion; that there might be desire for possession on his part, and a longing to be possessed on her part, and thereby the propagation of the specie would be continued. She must also be taught that when man loves, coaxes and caresses her, duty and the love she bears him, makes it incumbent upon her to grant his reasonable requests.

Every woman, before her marriage, must be fully instructed as to the consequences of the rite, that basically it is an expression of love, having for its consummation generation or regeneration; enjoyment under these conditions is not forbidden her, though she must be impressed with the important fact that the embrace should never be undertaken merely for the satisfaction of passion. Love must primarily be the incentive, then some great desire, whether this be for health, happiness, or long life, be firmly concentrated in the mind. Likewise must she be informed of the possibility of pain to be endured during the first, or first few, exercises of the creative function, because it is the birth of a new condition; the opening of a new world to her, though this is both natural and normal in every respect.

In addition it is necessary to impress on her mind the desirability of conserving her modesty, never to neglect her appearance and all that has charmed her husband; to observe propriety in the matter of dress and undress, and forever enshroud herself in a veil of mystery so that she will not become commonplace in his sight; apparently these are insignificant details, but upon them often depends continued happiness.

Instructions to the man are of equal importance if happiness is to be resultant of the union. He must be awakened to the absolutely uncontradictable fact that although he has considered himself lord of creation, there are a multitude of privileges belonging to him which he has *no* right to demand, though he may possess them if he can win them. It must be firmly impressed upon his mind that if he expects to retain a woman's love he must at all times respect her modesty; and should never attempt to uncover her unless she clearly indicates her desire; nor may he insist on the enjoyment of the sexual exercise, *especially on the wedding night,* but must win compliance by coaxing, caresses and loving attention; that failing, to deny himself such gratification—to be repaid many times for the sacrifice. He must be taught that a woman, even if she be his wife, may many times refuse his requests even though she herself desires the embrace; though by continuing his caresses without further requests, he can win her consent; however, he must use his reason in grasping a situation when she has cause for non-compliance, and cease his attention altogether for that time.

Very few young men come to the comprehension, until too late and her love has been destroyed, that in the beginning of marriage there may be far more suffering than pleasure for her and that she complies with his requests merely because of her love for him. It is at this time he must show the greatest care; brute force will induce in her a sense of loathing for him, while gentleness and sympathy will win her respect and bring him greater love.

An important lesson which *most* young men ever fail to learn is the fact that all normal women want and appreciate admiration of their person from their husbands. There is not a full-blooded woman living who does not feel that the man who professes to love her should likewise admire her form and think it beautiful; and if he fails to do this he will eventually regret his short-comings.

All men should quickly appreciate the fact that though the woman of his bosom comprehends little or nothing relative to the rights and privileges belonging to her, *she instinctively understands the art of love*. This feeling of, and longing for love, is inborn, and with her it is the open door to all she possesses. If she is offered love, she will reciprocate by giving of her all, by granting every desired privilege and willingly sacrifices herself as well as her honor. Woman is love personified, although this personification is frequently degraded. While he thinks of self, of achievements, of his business and the thousand and one other details of life, she thinks only of her love; this is the reason why his little attentions, his admiration, and caresses are so welcome and so highly treasured.

Man's life is his business. The most affectionate man living often appears to accept, through force of circumstances, love as merely a side issue. This is seldom because his love is less sincere and true than woman's, but because he is the protector of his home and the one upon whom devolves the necessity of supplying the needs of the family. In this he resembles the primitive man who often was obliged to leave wife and family for weeks at a time to secure the food they required; he did not deny himself their companionship because he wished to be free from them, but because necessity compelled him. Similarly the man of affairs must meet the keen competition of today and center his entire mind and whole attention on the achievement of success. Apparently he does not think of his wife, but deep in his consciousness there is an abiding love which manifests through his efforts to *accomplish for her sake.*

Should he at times forget the Regenerative Law of his being and request favors without the usual caresses, she must not hastily conclude that his love has waned or be foolish enough to accuse him of having in mind merely the gratification of his senses. This has led to countless disasters. Woman's intuition is usually correct if her personal feelings do not becloud it, and will tell her whether he really does not care, or that his action is merely an oversight of which *all* men are sometimes guilty. Although it may be necessary or advisable for her to call his attention to his seeming carelessness, she should be careful in her manner and not accuse him of deliberate neglect.

Another source of much sorrow, and possibly the destruction of his love for her, can readily be traced to opinions voiced, accusations made and slights offered by her when in certain erratic moods. If man is wise he will ignore these periods and every act and spoken word connected with them; thereby preserving his own happiness and peace of mind, and ultimately earning her gratitude for his consideration.

A common complaint of men to their friends and physician is, that their wives generally choose the time during the marriage rite to tell them of their faults and weaknesses, or accuse them of unfaithfulness. This practice is destructive to marital happiness and if continued is certain to create inharmony and mental unbalance. The one time in a man's life when he really desires peace and contentment is while in the love embrace; since it is during this period that the mind should be wholly free from all external and disturbing thoughts and be centered on some great desire in *addition* to that for love satisfaction. The woman who is foolish or ignorant enough to scold, find fault, or accuse during this sacred moment is certain to lose the love of her husband.

We offer no sympathy for the man who is vain enough to think he has the right to demand obedience from his wife relative to the embrace, and who fails to approach her with love and caresses; he does not manifest manhood, nor deserve the love of any good woman.

Without passion there can be no true and lasting love between the sexes, passion being the base of love. Granting this we emphatically state that there is no excuse for over indulgence of the passional nature. Love itself may be manifested at times **without the embrace;** and because a man caresses his wife daily is no reason he should that frequently be permitted indulgence in the marriage rite. There is a time and a season for all things. While there may be endearments and caresses whenever opportunity offers, exercise of the rite itself should not be sufficiently frequent to induce weakness; above all, it should never be undertaken while there is either ill feeling or a misunderstanding between the two; because this would poison mind and body and engender hatred one toward the other.

One of the most important things for the newly-married pair to learn is the necessity of controlling the passion if the union is to be a happy one. This has reference as much to the woman as to the man; the theory that woman is usually passionless being wholly wrong; when true, is regrettable. Youthful married people who have not been properly instructed in this respect are apt to fall into error and the embrace becomes a harmful habit rather than constructive exercise of the **creative** function. They must quickly realize that marriage does **not** give them the privilege of indulging to satiation; no individual has a right to such abuse and the marriage ceremony does **not** grant it.

It is the law in the creative realm that the more frequently the desire of the male is gratified the oftener will there be a call for indulgence. There should be a covenant between the twain, stipulating that the Rite may be indulged only so many times a week. If this is respected, their self-denial will be amply rewarded. We do not mean to infer that such a contract should be iron-clad and not occasionally broken, but should be the law of action.

While it is permitted them to derive pleasure from their act, *there must be a deeper and more holy object in view.* In the process of regeneration there is no actual waste of vital force even if the Rite is completed. If the embrace is indulged for any other purpose than generation, there should be *a full understanding between them to concentrate on some holy object or lofty ideal.* They should harmonize as nearly as possible, and the crisis of both should occur at the same time. The thought and the desire should be intensely held at the moment and it is well to draw up the breath and hold it during the exchange of living forces. If this is faithfully performed the vital energy in the seminal fluid will be absorbed by the intensity of the female organism and will electrify her entire body, just as the electric current charges the bar of steel that has previously been prepared for a magnet; while in the male the thought and retained breath will absorb the magnetic force in her lochia released by the glands of the vagina and uterus. We repeat, there is no waste, but a fair exchange which is resultant of peace, happiness and health.

There are very few people, irrespective whether married or single, who actually understand sexual laws; consequently it is rarely that the embrace is consummated as it should be. In most instances he indulges merely for pleasure; while poor she, remaining unaroused and simply the agent for his gratification, receives neither joy or strength; hence it is little wonder she comes to hate and despise the act and feels disgust at the mere mention of it. Because of this ignorance and selfishness the exercise is hardly ever performed in a divine and holy manner, and is one of the main causes for much of the dissatisfaction in married life.

If a man does not love a woman to the extent of wanting to caress and kiss her before he indulges in the Rite, and to continue to do so after the completion of the embrace, he does not really love her; the best that can be said, is, that he is impassioned by her. He has no right to request her favors; to do so is to prostitute his powers and energies.

The lover's kiss, like the creative exercise, has been much misunderstood and abused. It is as sacred in the sight of God as the marriage rite. The kiss is the symbol of true love, an emblem of affection; or , *it is the badge of hypocricy.* It is sanctioned only between those who love each other, between women who are good friends, and between relatives. Any other indulgence is damnable and destructive, because the same magnetic force exchanged between the pair during the sexual act also passes during the kiss; and it is readily understandable how undesirable it must be in instances where the kiss is exchanged between those who dislike each other, aye, even hate each other. Women are most frequently the lawbreakers. Who has not observed women kissing who were known to be bitter enemies? This is comparable to the famous Biblical kiss of Judas.

Another cause for the cooling of affection and that which was once intense love may often be traced to the general practice of continually sharing one bed. The married should sometimes occupy separate beds, and, when possible to arrange, often separate rooms; that modesty and privacy may be respected. The freedom often displayed in dressing and undressing is undesirable to the highest respect and love.

Those who live the married life thus far indicated will not be prudes; nor see anything in sex to be ashamed of. To them all that pertains to the creative function will be beautiful, holy, divine and a special blessing and privilege which a considerate God conferred upon his children; but they will also recognize that there is a time and a place for all things; that there are periods when he intensely wishes to see the beautiful outlines of the feminine form, and actually longs to "raise the veil," just as there is a time when *she desires* him to do this. If they always share the same room and the one bed, the "human form divine" becomes a common sight, nothing is left to the imagination of the god Love, and imagination once dead, love quickly follows the funeral.

Our experience teaches us that all who believe that sex is only for the gratification of the senses, who over-indulge and seldom, if ever, know a perfect union, having prostituted, debased and debauched the generative energy and so became abnormal, cannot see anything beautiful or divine in God's most mysterious creation. The happily married never belong to these classes.

Too often those entering the marital relation become careless as to dress and appearance. Both should continually strive to please each other in this respect, after, as before the ringing of the wedding bells. The woman may become careless of her appearance and the husband's imagination pictures a different woman than the one constantly appearing before him; the reaction has the potency to cool the intensity of his love for her. But woman is not alone the guilty party; he frequently becomes more careless than she. Before marriage he was a man in every respect; neat in appearance, gentlemanly in deportment. To continue in his former mode of living may seem too much trouble, but he must realize that her love means his happiness and should make every effort to retain it.

Love is the sum total of woman's life. Man is indeed foolish who ever attempts to change her attitude. There never can be any "settling down" in her case; she expects the days of courtship to continue *after* the wedding ceremony; those little favors, flowers, presents; pleasing speeches and little flatteries are always desired by the *real* woman. All of them are a part of her being; and irrespective of how prosaic or practical life may be, how many sorrows may be her share, these attentions are expected; comprising the foundation of her continued love for him; therefore should be gladly and freely granted by him in gentlemanly consideration, and not felt as arduous tasks.

The young wife, on her part, should constantly remember that with man conditions differ; he draws a line of distinction between love, passion, and business. Business is cold, calculating, and without emotion; foreign to a woman's nature. Whatever a woman becomes interested in, is based upon the emotion of either love or hate, and is the reason why she rarely forgives the fall of her own sex. She must never for a moment forget that *man can completely divorce passion and love,* that he can actually have passion for a woman without feeling any love for her, though he is not master enough to love a woman for whom he can feel no passion. In woman's sphere, except in rare cases, this is entirely different; although she may be passionate she will seldom allow her desires to be aroused unless she loves. Men and women are distinctly different from each other in their natures and to obtain happiness and avoid grievous mistakes which often lead to sorrow and unhappiness, they must not so judge each other according to their own nature.

Dr. P. B. Randolph, often termed the world's greatest philosopher of love, stated it as a law, that woman will forgive a man if he so far forgets himself as to have sexual congress with another woman, but will never pardon him if she learns he has been caressing, kissing, and loving her; because this last would be an affront to her own affectional nature, the base of her existence. On the contrary, a man may forgive his wife when guilty of infatuation for another man but will never do so if he knows her to be guilty of sexual embrace with another; because the existence of his being and his deepest love is founded in passion which he considers sacred and holy unto himself alone.

Another important truth which should be instilled into every young man, one he should never forget under penalty of forever losing the respect of a true woman who may love him, is this: that he must never, in her presence, or under any circumstances offering the possibility of having her informed of it, voice any coarse, common or slighting comment on her sex, or any function of woman. If she is true-hearted and loving, and we are considering only these, she expects, and rightly so, that he is a gentleman and considers every part of her being as beautiful and desirable. If ever he foolishly attempts any slighting allusion, no matter what the motive, to her creative organism, or any other part of her body, especially of her breasts, she will be so deeply wounded as to rarely, if ever, fully recover and again evince her former love for him.

The case of a little woman coming to us suffering from extreme nervousness, will partly illustrate this: We were well acquainted with both the young people before their marriage. She was a jolly little girl, a good companion, carefree and lovable. He more serious and apparently ignorant of the little weaknesses which make women lovable. They were married and for a time happy. After the birth of the first child, she lost some of her plumpness, especially the roundness of her breasts. On a certain occasion, just before the embrace, he foolishly made the remark that he did not like the appearance of her breasts as well now as he did before they were married. This cut her to the quick; causing her to brood over her loss, and inducing her to try every means in her power to regain her former symmetry, but all to no avail. The continual nursing of her wounded feelings finally resulted in a nervous ailment lasting for years and the expenditure of much money. After consulting many physicians without relief, (and it must be here mentioned, he loved her deeply enough to make every effort to find relief for her,) she came to us, confessing the cause for all her trouble. It required some little time and effort to convince her that merely because he had foolishly told her he liked her better, or preferred her with her former appearance, did not in the least imply that he loved her less; that as an actual truth he might even love her more when in this plight, because of his sympathy; what a man "liked" and what he actually "loved" being two entirely different things; as is readily shown by the self-evident fact that a man likes to see his wife well and strong, but may dearly love her even though she is seriously ill. Once fully convinced of her erroneous interpretation of his statements, she made every effort to forget the incident, and within two months was entirely free of the nervous affliction, and her jolly self again.

The Great Madness

WOULD NATIONALIZE CUPID

"Washington, August 21, 1920. The nationalization of Cupid is being proposed by influential women.

"They are mothering a movement to have a United States Bureau of Matrimony established to promote the eugenic marriage of young people and to bring together lonely hearts of all ages.

"When Congress meets, efforts will be made to have a bill providing for such a bureau introduced, according to announcement today by Miss Fannie Wolfson, secretary of the Woman's United States Chamber of Commerce, of which Mrs. Howard Gould is head.

"There is no reason, she says, why romance stamped with the official O. K. of the U. S. A., should not be as attractive as the other kind.

"A Government matrimonial bureau, as we plan it, would promote eugenic matings, but would be conducted in such a manner as to encourage romance. At the head of it should be a woman of experience and wisdom, who is human enough to understand the problems of young people."—*Evening Bulletin, Philadelphia, August 21, 1920.*

The universal question daily propounded by those who regret the decadence of the race is: Why is there no longer respect for the law? Easily answered! Because so many of the American people, especially women, who, shirking their duty to the family, devote their time to the advocation of imbecillic laws;

that now all legislation is coming to be considered for no other purpose than defiance.

We believe in eugenics, but laws governing marriage eugenically are not only useless, they are destructive? Why? Because two people who, loving each other and aspiring to parentage, can become the procreators of physical giants and mental geniuses, even though they themselves are far from healthy; while two people physically strong and mentally brilliant, and whose marriage would be universally encouraged by such an official, but *heart and soulless bureau,* would frequently become the parents cf weaklings, imbeciles, and perverts. Why? Because in this instance love not being the base of the marital relationship, they prostitute themselves body and soul, and children born to them are unwanted.

When men and women attain to that state of wisdom and understanding permitting them to test the *love two people bear toward each other,* then such a bureau will become a constructive, rather than a destructive, agency.

Dangerous Period of Life

PUBERTY

Puberty is that period in the life of a girl when her procreative organism has reached the development necessary to function as required by Nature for the conception of a new being. Undoubtedly, Nature had primarily intended that when this stage was reached she should have attained full bodily growth, and be prepared to do her full duty as a mother.

Unhappily, the laws governing the development of the body have not kept apace with those giving life and activity to the creative functions, and at this age it is possible for almost any girl to conceive, three or five years before she is fully grown.

Because of this anomaly the physical structure is that of a girl who should be happy with her dolls or in the companionship of boys and girls, while the mind and desires are those of a fully developed woman, and herein we find the difficulty to keep her innocent of acts which would be wholly to her detriment in later life. On this account the period of puberty is most dangerous, and every care must be exercised by the guardian or mother that there be no misstep, resulting in a ruined life.

A few months before puberty we have a girl who is wholly carefree, happy, and unconscious in the companionship of boys; taking part in their games and all their sports, possibly failing to recognize there is a difference between the sexes; then, almost unperceptibly there is a change; a transformation of her entire being taking place; the mental attitude is no longer that of a boyish-girl, but quickly becomes that of the woman. With the awakening of the sex activity life appears totally different from what it seemed but a short time before; painful consciousness takes the place of the former instinctive activity. The girl may be likened to the uncouth youth, who is aware there *is* a correct way to enter a room filled with people but who is ignorant of how to proceed; the greater his effort, the more fruitful of error. The girl is fully conscious that the former carefree associations with boys and girls indiscriminately can no longer be continued, but she is unenlightened of just what is the proper thing to do, and how to do it.

Long before this period in the girl's life the wise mother will have informed her exactly what to expect, when and how to expect it. Generally this information is gained from associates or older persons ignorant of the true facts, and here is the fruitful source to which can be traced much of the illness and misery responsible for the suffering of so many women.

Often the girl is wholly ignorant and does not expect any change, then before she is aware of it, she is confronted with a flow of blood that she cannot reconcile with anything except an internal wound or rupture, and in the paralyzing effect this unexpected phenomena has on her mind she is incapable of clear thought; merely reasoning that her parents would not comprehend were she to tell them of the occurrence. Thrown on her own resources, she reasons from past experience; is aware that whenever there is a flow of blood the first thing to look for is a cloth and *cold* water; she secures this, applying the cold water until the flow ceases, thereby laying the foundation for future illness.

Had she been instructed in anatomy and physiology and the natural functions of the creative organism, and told that at a certain period of her life the ovaries prepare the ovum or human egg; that preceding the passage of this ovum from the ovary discharging to the uterus *via* the Fallopian tubes, where it may be impregnated and become a human, there is a flow of mucous and blood preparing the passage; that this blood will be discharged from the vagina, she would be prepared for the phenomena.

Moreover, almost any mother can anticipate this event; the action of her daughter clearly indicating its advent. The symptoms most often manifesting, are various mental peculiarities; due to the physiological foundation of menstruation resting in the nervous system; thus affecting the entire nervous system and reflecting this on the mental faculties through erratic activity. The appetite is frequently irregular; on the contrary, there may be a craving for food clearly not desirable. Often there is great languor, backache, pain in various parts of the body, chills, headache, morbidity, perversity of action and irritability.

When such symptoms are evident in the girl of ten to fourteen years of age the mother should be prepared with her sanitary cloths, and kindly inform the daughter that at the first symptom of the unusual, to come to her that she may be fully prepared for what is the greatest event in her life.

Finally, when the expected symptoms appear, the girl should be induced to retire to her room and bed or recline on a couch; common remedies, according to the symptoms manifesting, prescribed. If there should be chills and slight feverishness, the hot teas given until these symptoms disappear and the flow becomes normal, when the girl should be allowed to remain quiet for several days. *If the inception of the menstrual flow of the girl is anticipated, properly prepared for, and correctly taken care of, it at once removes the cause of future trouble.* The menses once naturally established, becomes a normal function of the female organism and seldom the cause of trouble.

How vastly different from the usual occurrence! We have in mind a case that will clearly illustrate this. A family of four; two boys and two girls; the mother an average American, who had been taught nothing when a girl and whose only knowledge was her own experience; taking it for granted that just as she had to learn so must her daughters. The older of the two girls, at the age of thirteen and while romping and playing with her brothers and several neighborhood boys, suddenly became aware that conditions were not as usual with her. There appeared nothing unusual in so far as her physical well-being was concerned but, as she expressed it, "something cold seemed to flow." Almost unconsciously she placed her hand to the mouth of the vagina, and, on withdrawing, found it covered with blood. Naturally, she was dumbfounded and did not know what move to make; in this dilemma she turned to her companions who were as ignorant, and happily, as innocent as she. The concurrent conclusion arrived at by the consultation, was, that the best thing to do was to secure a cloth and cold water; that possibly it was no more than an ordinary nosebleed with which they were familiar. The cloth and cold water was secured and applied, with the result that the flow ceased and a chill set in, the child having been perspiring freely due to its exercise. When the time for the next periodical flow arrived there was no indication of it, but instead a chill and swelling of the limbs. A physician was consulted, who suspected something out of the ordinary; questioned the girl until she informed him of the former occurrence. For many years thereafter this girl suffered severely at each monthly period, all due to the ignorance of the mother.

Occurrences of this nature are well nigh universal and certainly does not say much for our twentieth century enlightenment and our boast of being intelligently informed on all important subjects. It is certainly not an honor to us to be forced to admit that more than nine-tenths of our girls reach the age of puberty without the slightest knowledge of the phenomena of life before them. Nor is it an honor to motherhood, that girls, because of their ignorance, should attempt to hide, for fear of unjust accusations, what every girl should look forward to with as great a pride as the young man does to his first long trousers—an emblem of womanhood on her part, on his, a symbol of manhood.

Not all motherhood is based on ignorance. We have in mind a mother of the enlightened age; one blessed with several daughters who do her honor. She is not merely the human machine who prepares their food and looks after their clothing— she is also their companion. Just as these girls come to their mother with their studies, so do they go to her with their confessions, seeking information. If Johnny Jones happens to display his wisdom of the world and gives expression to some remark they do not understand, they appeal to their mother for an interpretation. She, wise mother, instead of showing self-consciousness on her part and telling them to be ashamed to repeat "such a nasty remark," tells them just what he did mean and then proceeds to give them a full explanation of it in language chaste and pure. These girls never ask a companion for an explanation of a remark they do not understand, they await the evening, then appeal to the mother, who, as will be universal in the good time coming, is also their confessor.

The girls have been instructed in biology, anatomy and physiologly, they comprehend the mysteries of creation; and have been told of the coming event when they will bid good-bye to childhood and enter girlhood.

One of the girls, complaining of flushes and a feeling of dizziness, was promptly kept home from school so she might rest. Informing the mother of the appearance of a discharge, she was shown how to apply the sanitary cloth; how to change it; and taught the correct method of bathing locally with warm water, as also the sponging of the entire body with tepid water once each day.

Instead of sending the girl to school the next day, she was allowed to remain home and rest, thus freeing the mental and nervous system from the strain always resultant on forced study during this trying time. This mother never allows her daughters to attend school during these periods, but tells them to rest, play games, have music, and to generally enjoy themselves. What is the result? The development of these girls is at its best; there is no nervous irritability; no irrational action; no morbidity; they are jolly and carefree, and seldom are aware of the periodic flow, other than the necessity of changing cloths, and keeping the body free from undesirable odors. This is an enlightened, twentieth century mother.

Our educational system is fundamentally wrong and destructive in its tendency. It is diametrically contrary to the laws governing normal boyhood and girlhood; laws that should be well understood by every physician and educator:

First: Boys during adolescence are extremely active and, to develop normally, must be continually occupied with exercises, recreations, and studies, so that by the hour for retiring they are sufficiently tired to want sleep. This routine will be a preventive against habits, frequently the curse of boyhood and the cause of weakness in later life.

Second: The physiologic base of menstruation resting in the nervous system; it is necessary, if the welfare of the girl is considered, that a directly opposite method of procedure be followed in her consideration. Instead of urging her to be active and to intensive study, as we should do with the boys, it is essential to as nearly as possible allow her complete rest during this four or five-day period, nor dare we induce her to difficult mental activity either directly before or after, the monthly period.

Our present system is to consider boys and girls during adolescence and puberty as exactly alike in their natures, desires, tendencies, mental capacity and physical endurance, when as previously stated, they are directly the opposite, and the treatment accorded them must be diametrically different if good is to result. This cannot be successfully contradicted. In the name of reason and common sense, how then can we expect a healthy womanhood and normal motherhood when we accord the girls in school the treatment we should only prescribe for the boys, so completely shattering their entire nervous system, weakening the mentality, and breaking down the moral stamina?

At the time of the transition from girlhood to womanhood other radical changes take place. Instead of continuing her companionship with the boys as formerly, hugging and kissing them, and taking part in all their games, she becomes shy and self-conscious, no longer the jolly good fellow and happy playmate. The boys cannot comprehend this change in her attitude, and often she becomes the subject of their jests; irritating and creating in her an abnormal sensitiveness; leading to permanent injury which is avoidable if she is properly instructed as to what to expect in herself.

At this juncture her imagination begins to unfold; the creative nature also asserts itself. She becomes conscious of desires within herself formerly unknown; has as yet no comprehension of love and may not for many years, but has intuitively a knowledge that there exists that which would give her pleasure and a feeling of satisfaction; *the womanly longing to be possessed.* This is intensified when in the presence of a male companion whom she respects; she has approached the brink of the dangerous period in her life; and unless she is fully prepared, is liable to commit serious errors.

For instance, if in company with a man or youth she likes, and who is not thoroughly honorable, she may easily be aroused; her desires becoming so pronounced that she readily condescends to comply with his wishes and so enter the rank of unwilling, unconscious, and unhappy motherhood, though innocent in thought and intent. If this happens society discards and condemns her, when in truth she is as innocent before God as the day she was born; those whose duty it was to instruct and prepare her, alone being guilty.

Besides instructing our girls in sexology, we must enlighten them as to the many and varied changes that will take place in their innermost being and how to bravely meet these and overcome them by constant occupation, exercise, games, bathing, social intercourse, recreation, music, plays free from morbid and immoral suggestions, and how to avoid having the passions aroused beyond control. If our duty is well performed, we need have little fear for their safety.

The Eternal Feminine

Let every man, young or old, ever remember the great law—that to woman love is her entire existence; her duty and her obedience having their foundation in her affections. She is seldom capable of drawing a distinction; either loves or hates, and all of life judged accordingly.

Dangerous Period of Life
(Continued)

Menopause

As at puberty the temple doors of the creative being are opened that God's universe may be peopled, so at Menopause are they closed and Nature bespeaks the Benediction: "As thou hast been faithful despite all thy suffering, now mayst thou know the joys of life without the shadow of fear."

The period of a woman's fruitful years are varied. In some instances menstruation may commence as early as nine and ten years and continue until the age of fifty; while in others the lunar season does not appear until the fifteenth or even the eighteenth year; ceasing at thirty-five to thirty-eight. Many conditions influence both the commencement and the cessation. Heredity often governs and a girl whose mother did not change from girlhood to womanhood before she was fifteen, may expect the same rule to recur in her case, though this is not always true.

Women who have borne children generally do not enter the Menopause as early in life as those who have not; and the more children a woman has given birth to, the later will be the appearance of the "Change of Life."

A fallacy which has been universally accepted as a truth and which we hope to free suffering womanhood from, is the race belief that when a woman approaches the years when Menopause should occur, she will commence to suffer all the misery, both physical and mental, that the flesh is heir to. Nothing could be further from the truth; physical ailments and mental morbidity are not at all necessary; and when present merely indicate either ignorance or an abnormal life.

Admittedly, at this period of life the creative organism does undergo a change; the ovaries atrophying; reducing in size, and ceasing to function in the same manner they did previously. It is also generally believed that the uterus, like the ovaries, will atrophy; no doubt this is true in the majority of instances, *but is entirely unnecessary and if the law governing its life and activity is understood, women will remain as youthful in their passions and possibility to exchange the full love embrace with their husbands, after as before, and one of the chief causes for divorces because of the wife's frigidity, will be removed.*

During the period when Menopause takes place the entire nervous system must undergo a thorough adjustment; and one of the first symptoms of the approach of a normal change of life is irregularity in menstruation. Sometimes the lunar flow will be missed for several months, then may appear regularly for some time; again ceasing for a shorter or longer period; this continues until the process of reconstruction is completed.

Undoubtedly even in the strongest women who have lived in obedience with natural laws, the various changes require greater strength than did the monthly periods of cleansing and because of this, the food should be especially vitalizing and free from congesting material, while the body should have less active exercise and the mind longer hours of rest.

Teaching by illustration is much the easiest method. We recall the case of an average woman who during her youth received no instructions in the care of her physical organism, and who refused to accept opportunities since for gaining this important knowledge. She is the mother of several children; suffered severely in giving birth to most of them, by reason of improper food, worry, over-work, and many other unnatural and unnecessary factors. She is now in her fourth year of the change. A day or two before the commencement of the flow there is a disturbance of the stomach, then a bilious headache so severe it becomes necessary for her to go to bed, this may continue twenty-four to forty-eight hours, and during this time she is practically unable to see on account of the suffering; now the flow of an odorous fluid commences and continues for possibly five to six days. The woman is irritable, at times extremely nervous, and next to irrational. From present appearance the change will not be completed for another year or two. Our experience indicates that, with slight variations, this is the usual "hell of middle life" through which women pass.

We have in mind an acquaintance, a woman who was blessed with an enlightened mother by whom she was fully instructed during her girlhood years. This lady no longer believes that she need be ashamed of any portion of her body; feels that she has a perfect right to be proud of it. She has long since thrown into the discard the age old idea that she is the plaything of her husband, with no right to refuse his request, or indicate her desires; as also the belief that when she has passed through the gates of the Menopause she will be no longer a desirable companion for her husband, and incapable of offering him the pleasures of youth.

This lady, the mother of nine children, at the age of forty-eight, had neither a thought nor an indication of the approaching crisis until the lunar flow ceased to appear. A day or two after the period when menstruation should have commenced she was aware of slightly hot flushes and a desire to rest. Instead of commencing to worry, woman's usual companion, she took a warm douche, a tepid bath with a quick rub, a hot cup of tea and hied herself to bed. In a few hours these flushes passed and she felt wide-awake, though slightly nervous; in place of asking for an opiate, she dressed and took a long walk, swinging her arms and breathing deeply; and for the next few days changed her diet to luscious fruits and fresh green vegetables, such as lettuce, celery, corn, peas; and plenty of milk and fresh eggs. During the time of what had formerly been the lunar season she abstained from meats, sweets, spices and stimulating drinks.

The next periodical flow appeared as usual, but she continued the former treatment. After an intermittent appearance for about a year, the flow ceased entirely and for six months past there has been no indication of it ever again appearing.

Cases vary even when an enlightened regime is faithfully followed, though it is safe to say that every abnormal and undesirable symptom can be quickly overcome by rest, abstaining from certain foods, taking proper exercise and a correct outlook on life.

Generally the greatest enemies woman must contend with during the Menopause are indigestion, dyspepsia, sluggishness of the liver, over-work, abnormal indulgence, unhygienic surroundings, and various other causes. If these be removed and normal habits of life established, there need be no reason for worry.

A race belief which has been the cause of more misery, sorrow, broken hearts and disrupted homes, than almost all other combined influences, is the universally accepted delusion that with the cessation of the periodic flow, woman naturally ceases to enjoy the embraces of her husband, and is no longer capable of conferring upon him the former satisfaction; supposedly due to the atrophying of the uterus, and shrinkage of the vaginal walls.

This thought, always present in the mind of woman long before the time of the approaching change, has been as a "thorn in the flesh," as every woman looked forward to the period when the fires-of-love in her would no longer burn and she become incapable to give her wanted pleasure to the man she loved, with the altogether natural expectation that he would seek elsewhere than at his own fireside.

This constant fear and expectation unquestionably has had much to do with the atrophying of the uterus and the shrinking of the vaginal walls, as well as with the gradual deadening of her desire for the usual love embrace, until by the time the "change of life" had actually been completed, her entire organism, as also her desires and capabilities, had become paralyzed and she showed a frigidity of nature totally at variance with her former self.

There comes to us the psychological law expressed in the Bible as a religious truth: "The thing thou feared has come upon thee" and nowhere else in Nature is the working of the law more certain than in the domain of the emotional nature.

As a matter of absolute—and saving—truth, we can assure every woman living that there is no foundation in fact, in this destructive race belief; that she may not merely avoid becoming a victim of this inertia, but that she can, if she will, become many times more capable of both experiencing and giving affectional pleasure *after* the Menopause, than during any other period of her life, with the possible exception of the first few times she permitted the embrace.

If a woman will keep the affectional fires burning during the period while passing through the change of life by *willing, and with conscious thought, accepting the conjugal embrace two to three times each week between the lunar periods, being watchful that she experiences the complete crisis in its highest perfection each time, she will not only keep alive and fully awakened the love nature, but she will prevent the atrophying process of the uterus and the shrinkage of both uterus and the vaginal walls; becoming thereby capable of giving more intense and prolonged pleasure to her spouse than ever before, because the constant fear of pregnancy will be entirely removed.*

If we can be successful in spreading this *law of nature* broadcast so that all women may come to an understanding of its potency for the continued retention of youth, then countless homes that would otherwise be laid in ruin, will continue happy and content in the knowledge that all is well.

Let every woman look forward for a greater fulfillment of life *after* the Menopause, giving extra care and attention to the entire system while passing through the change; keeping alive the entire being, mind, body and soul, by recreation; the mental faculties awake and active, the body virile through exercise. Let them attend good plays, associate with refined, cheerful women, never mentioning the change that is taking place, and consistently refusing to look upon the morbid side of life; eating only those foods which will build up the mental and nervous system, creating vital forces, so maintaining equilibrium.

Like with the girl entering womanhood who should be prohibited from intensive study and hard work, so should the woman entering Menopause be forbidden the activity she had previously enjoyed; the system requiring an extra supply of nerve energy at this period of life; if this vital force is lacking invalidism may be her portion during the rest of her life. Very often a woman at this time is like a ship at sea during a storm, carrying a heavy load. If she is to hold to her course and safely reach port, speed must be reduced, that there may be a reserve of power.

The change having taken place, she no longer requires the extra strength and vitality previously necessary for her well-being; nor will she need to recover the loss sustained every month by the lunar flow; thus will she be stronger, capable of greater effort, and possess the power of showing deeper affection for her husband.

A serious error of the past, and one still prevalent, is the generally accepted opinion believed by most women, that Menopause is a disease, an evil from which there is no escape. Undoubtedly they have had sufficient reason for such a conclusion because of the fact that women who previously seemed to enjoy health and strength, no sooner commenced with the change of life, when they would suffer from various ailments, all more or less serious.

Menopause is an entirely natural functional change; instead of heralding disease, misery, and not infrequently death, it should be the advance agent of health and strength, a time for the enjoyment of the fruits of the past life.

During the change of life, any latent weakness that had not actively manifested previously, may exhibit itself when the system is unprepared for the extra strain. Instead of seeking the actual cause, usually to be found in lack of exercise, indulgence in congesting foods, overwork, insanitary conditions, destructive surroundings, the Menopause is blamed for it, when in fact it has nothing whatever to do with the present suffering other than possibly furnishing an avenue for its manifestation.

The change of life should not be a cause for fear and dread, but looked forward to as a means for greater peace and contentment. If harmony has previously been established in the system, Menopause will proceed normally and the body obtain freedom from many of its former weaknesses. One fact cannot be too strongly impressed upon the mind of every woman, namely; that if afflicted with what is usually termed "female weakness," they will suffer more or less during the change, and should hardly expect that it will be a cure-all, or the means of freeing them from these ailments; may even intensify the condition; establishing chronic invalidism, hysterical, nervous, or irrational moments; making life miserable for themselves and members of the family.

The Absolute Law

One of the great laws that *must* be obeyed, if health, happiness, and peace is the aim of life, is absolute faithfulness to one mate and perfect purity in the exercise of the creative function. The correct, pure, and holy exercise of this energy is the *key* to race redemption and personal Immortalization; while its abuse is the open door to degeneracy, misery, and war, the Path of Death.

The Path of Death

"The Soul That Sinneth It Shall Die."

How many of the uncountable denizens of earth who have read the Bible, and consciously or unconsciously desire to be known as Christians, have given a careful study of the books of Moses, wherein he emphatically commands man *not* to "cast his seed upon the ground." How many who have studied the law actually obey it in its spirit?

Of all those who have read, or have heard read, this fiat, very few fully realize its great significance to the entire race; actually comprehending it to be the fundamental law of life and death. Disobedience to this one command by the multitudes has produced war and rumor of war, sin and sickness, misery and death; in fact, all the undesirable conditions which enslave mankind, making of the earth life a hell, whereas it might just as readily be a place of joy and happiness.

"The soul that sinneth it shall die," and "cast not thy seed upon the ground," have one and the same significance and apply to all the abuses of man's power of generation and *re*-generation. In the ultimate it is immaterial by what specific act or acts he casts his seed upon the ground; whether he be married and living in prostitution with his legalized wife; committing solitary vices; Sodomism; the Rite of Gomorrah, or any one of the other unspeakable practices; the result is the same with but the slight difference that one act is possibly more beastly than the other. For instance, Sodomism is far more degrading in the very thought than the acts indulged in by men and women who, assuming the marriage rite, fail to bring to a successful conclusion that sacred act because of fear that children may result; and through such disobedience of the *first* Divine Law is engendered hatred one against the other; disease and sorrow, misery and ultimately death.

It is the universal disobedience to the commands voiced by Moses that is directly responsible for most of the misery in the world. Men and women continually prostitute themselves; draining the very life forces; casting them aside as so much rubbish, that a carnal passion may be satisfied; a moment's pleasure enjoyed; though the result is always more moral weakness, physical and mental degradation. Contrary to all that has been taught by those who fail to clearly comprehend the subject, we maintain that the sex appetite is not abnormal, not a potency which came to man gradually as he fell from his high estate. "Male and female created He them," hence there were the creative organism of the male as of the female, and God did not create these for the mere satisfaction of having accomplished the theretofore unknown, but because He *intended them for a noble purpose—procreation and recreation;* and it is unreasonable and illogical to believe that desire was not given man and woman at the same moment of creation; because *where desire is unknown use is not made of a potency or principle.* We therefore condemn and exclude those unreasonable inculcations which would have us believe the creative desire did not come to man until after he had *fallen* from his high estate.

It is instructions such as these that induce people to believe sex longing to be unnatural and unholy; causing them to attempt suppression, so stifling natural impulse and creating an abnormal condition, generally ending in degrading vices and indulgence in soul-searing rites and debauches.

We firmly contend there is nothing impure in the entire department of sex; nor unnatural in the normal desire; though **freely** admitting there may be unsanctioned exercise of the creative function; ending in sorrow, misery, and ultimately in death. It is the degradation to which the function is subjected that is objectionable, not the potency itself. One must be reasonable and differentiate right use and its desirable results, from abuse and non-use and the penalty which sin returns.

We emphatically condemn the inimical teachings that creative desire is destructive to the spiritual nature in man. As a fact, the contrary is true; although it must be clearly understood the appetite be normal and indulgence not merely for pleasure; the selfish passion be in strict abeyance, while the purpose of the Rite be either generation or re-generation, though there is no sin in the ecstacy that accompanies a "deed well done."

Because of the pernicious teachings, leading the public to the belief that normal sex desire is destructive to the spiritual nature in man, many follow the Path of Death. On the one hand we have those who attempt to kill out all desire, thereby destroying the *source* of power in man—the foundation of his spiritual regeneration and redemption; while on the other hand are the advocates of license and unbridled passion; giving free rein to their passions in promiscuous relationship and free love —damning the soul and making moral lepers of such.

The strength of the creative energy is to the human being as steam is to the engine; the greater the amount of steam the more power; provided always, it is forced along the proper channels and held under control. Similarly, the stronger the creative power in man, when combined with normal desire, the greater are his possibilities for achievement; provided, also, the power is directed along the right channels—for generation and re-generation.

That sex or creative desires are normal throughout *all* Nature, is clearly indicated by the animal, which though not seeking mating at all times, does seek the satisfaction of Nature's fulfillment when in season. This cannot be termed the carnal nature; but rather the creative nature within the animal, which, at certain seasons, awakens in order to perpetuate its specie. Many writers and educators do not seem to grasp the difference between Man and animal; failing to take into consideration the fact that the animal seeks satisfaction *during* the lunar period, while the human seeks either before or after the Moon's rule. With animals the law governing the period when conception may take place is from one to seven days; after this time the male seldom approaches the female and if he does, she fights him. The contrary is true in the realm of humanity; the human male would not think of requesting the favor while the woman is under Luna's sway and thereafter conception may take place for a period of from one to ten days; then follows the time when all the forces may be employed for *regeneration*.

That which carnal desire has been unable to accomplish in the animal, it has in the human—the diabolical reasoning which induces the male to leave the female when masculine passion is satisfied, or at the request of the female. It is *not* because of his creative desires that man has become degraded to a degree lower than the beast, but through the abominable and degrading practices by which he attempts to sate his appetites.

Truth is frequently unpleasant to hear, especially is this so when sex is the problem under consideration. However, if we are men and women, and not merely males and females— weaklings and degenerates, we will use our reasoning faculties and give careful consideration to the subject from every prospective.

The normal, healthy man selects a time for all things; and though he may be one of the most virile men in the universe, he would not think of attempting to satisfy his desire except at the proper time; if he does, it is clearly an indication of either ignorance or weakness, or of some diseased condition lurking within. Generally we partake of three meals a day; this becomes a habit and we have a sense of hunger at certain times each day; having no need of mentally dwelling on the subject. We pursue our business, vocation, or profession with neither thought nor desire for food except at the proper time. In like manner the healthy man gives his attention to the work before him and does not allow his mind to dwell on carnal satisfaction. When the "time is propitious" he seeks his mate and in holiness exchanges the embrace with her. This is Nature's method.

Sad, indeed, to contemplate the many who live to eat and drink, and the more numerous who even depend on drugs and salines to free the body of the surplus food, to again indulge the depraved appetite. These are on a par with the man who exercises his creative powers, stopping short of the actual *crisis;* incompleting the Rite, that he may shortly again enjoy the carnal pleasure; these find, in the end, that they have wasted the life principle, not by "casting the seed upon the ground" but through the repeated shocks to the nervous system, and shortly to be left without the power even to enjoy.

For the true man, love must be the actuating force; the true, normal, and healthy male never for a moment considers it possible or desirable to mate with a woman for whom he has neither affection or love. With primitive man there was but one consideration, and the object in view was procreation; he had not as yet attained to the knowledge of the human soul; of the possibility of its immortalization; nor had he reached spiritual conception.

There may have been love in his breast for his mate and a desire for children; but beyond this his reasoning faculties did not go; it is even possible that as in the animal kingdom of today, his mate, having only a certain period during which she sought embrace; the male knowing no other law than that of obedience to her wish. We no longer belong to the primitive ancestors, although in some respects we are less civilized, if civilization is based on morality and spirituality. We have the power of reasoning; the comprehension and understanding that there is in man more than can be satisfied by eating, drinking, sleeping, and a pleasurable act through which procreation is possible; we feel within ourselves that we are dual; that while we have a desire to live and enjoy, and to give pleasure, we are constantly seeking the ideal and longing for an understanding of the laws which will lead us into the Great Beyond. All of this the primitive man missed; therefore it is entirely illogical to reason creative impulses and potencies from his standpoint.

Unquestionably there is much that moderns might do well to accept as examples after which to pattern life. For instance, the primitive man was well satisfied with the affection of one woman; on this account his passions did not become inflamed as happens at present when men indulge promiscuously, absorbing mixed *lochia,* as they partake of mixed food and drink. This is always destructive to health and peace of mind; for the scientific reason that when men or women attempt to embrace, or be embraced, in the marriage rite, with more than one person within a limited time, the entire blood becomes infused, or charged, with a mixed magnetic force, always exchanged during the creative act. This creates a consuming fire in the blood; a continuous desire for indulgence; producing an irritation of the sexual organism; inducing the victim to seek embrace after embrace, until tuberculosis or impotence is the result. The active life of the girl of the street is at most but five years; the destructive fires within, constantly fed, is the cause.

Furthermore, our primitive ancestors *lived* in harmony with the greatest of all laws; the one so consistently inculcated by Moses, through which he attempted to save his people from the fearful diseases which were ravaging them; having their inception in continuous indulgence to the point of satisfaction, and then discontinuing for the moment; thereby cheating themselves, their female victims, and God's greatest law; damning themselves and those guilty with them.

The great mass of men have not yet become cognizant of the absolute law, that man has not the slightest right, even though married, to embrace the woman unless he does it in love. To seek the embrace when passion and desire, minus love, is the incentive, is to commit a diabolical act; it is prostitution; resulting in mutual hate, sex degeneracy ending in impotency; and if a child be the result, it may be a weakling, an idiot, or with tendencies to crime or insanity.

The sex function with all its potentialities is the highest and greatest gift presented by God to man, because He desired the lesser creation to be co-workers with Him. The creative power in man peoples the earth with His children; it enables man to gradually manifest immortality; it is a potent factor for continued youth, health, beauty, and longevity; while the abuse of the function is the cause, now as always, of all the plagues that have appalled humanity. If one is seeking for a vivid picturization of the results of these abuses, he but need read the Biblical narratives of Moses with his children in the wilderness, threatened with extinction of the race; saved only through the discontinuance of "casting the seed upon the ground" —the symbolic *raising of the serpent.*

Correct use of any potency, assuming that this includes normal use, is the *only* method to greater power; while the abuse of any potential inheritance produces a gradual weakening and ultimate destruction, the dissipation of that power. Especially is this true regards all pertaining to sex.

Another law governing man in his relationship with woman and entirely separate from those already mentioned, is of equal importance if he aspires to reach his highest development. While it is indisputable that the *greatest* consideration that should govern the embrace is *love,* it is equally true that he must approach her only by gaining her consent, preparing her through caresses and the endearments so highly prized by every true and normal woman. No man has any right to possess a woman until he has first aroused her to an active desire to be possessed; and many a woman considered as frigid, or actually almost dormant in feeling, may be aroused to the heights of the love passion by well directed caresses. The basis of all sex relationship *must* be mutual consent sanctioned by love.

We condemn, to the full extent of our power, the practice of countless men, termed husbands, taking forcible possession of their wedded partners, considering them bound to comply because of a marriage certificate; this constitutes rape in the spiritual sense, just as surely as when man attempts to use force on other women than his wife.

White slavery so universally condemned is not a bit worse and no greater cause of sorrow and misery than is the prostitution continually practiced between countless men and women, who, though married, have no love for each other, and who, in many instances, actually hate each other. A white slave is one who, contrary to her desires, is made a prisoner and is forced to receive attentions which are repulsive to her, until finally she is willing to lead an immoral life without compulsion. Where is there any actual difference betwen the woman of "ill fame" who sells her body, and the husbanded lady who, for one reason or another permits favors revolting to her nature and while possibly hating or bearing malice toward her husband? Not alone will the woman suffer, he, also, is severely punished; the incentive may be different, the ultimate results are identical.

We have proclaimed that woman, especially those married, have become slaves to the passions of their husbands; but what of the numberless instances where husbands truly love their wives, obeying the laws in their entirety, never approaching them except with caresses and consent, but who, time and again, are allowed the privilege only under condition that a promise is made to be "careful?" Plainly stated, only after he agrees to "cast his seed upon the ground," thereby *protecting* her, thus committing the crime which Moses forbade all people under penalty of death to the Soul. Foolish he! Because he loves and desires, complies with her request, only to find that for some unknown reason, she becomes less lovable and more irritable; harder to please, more unsatisfied and fault-finding; while he comes to care less for her and finds himself gradually losing strength, and finally condemning the marriage rite. This is the Path to Death.

The Path of Death

(Continued)

Sex perversion, the path leading to death, seems to be in itself a perversion, like a dream within a dream; one of its various manifestations being the white slave traffic, organized not so much because of the demand for women to be exploited for immoral purposes, as upon the want for young and innocent girls by men rich in this world's goods, who have become so thoroughly satiated with the more common abuses of the sex functions that they continually hunger for something out of the ordinary. Most of these men are actually accepted in their own community as examples of morality and uprightness, nevertheless, in their secret life are the directing cause of countless youthful victims being trapped and initiated into a life of beastliness and brutality, the prey of perverted beasts, mistakenly termed men. Unfortunately, it is not alone elderly men who attain such a degree of degradation; the practice is encouraged extensively by young men with abnormal tendencies, usually the sons of the wealthy, who can amply afford the expense incurred.

How to remedy this destructive and demoralizing condition is the great problem confronting us; which must be solved, and the remedy applied, if the Nation is to be redeemed from the disintegration it is daily undergoing; sex perversion indulged by a large percentage of people surely leading to the crumbling of the foundation stones of human society. History, time and again, informs us that when sex degeneracy becomes universal, it dooms the Nation honeycombed by it; being a cancer of malignant growth eating away the heart of the people; always in the past having been the main cause of the downfall of the great nations of earth.

In seeking for the cause of this degeneracy, and willing to accept the truth when we are confronted with it, we will soon learn that generally the parents of sons with perverted tastes are themselves deeply guilty of infringing upon Creative laws; possibly the child was undesired, therefore cursed in thought throughout the days of the mother's pregnancy. Admittedly, it is not always the fault of one or both of the parents, that the child becomes a pervert; but the exceptions are not the rule; and even in the isolated cases it will be found that, like the inheritance of syphilis, the tendencies may have been inherited from grandparents or even great-grandparents.

The remedy that will dispel the ignorance pervading humanity relative to the creative function, necessitates the constant inculcation of the *sacredness of sex,* and the observance of creative laws as a *religious duty essential to the salvation of the soul;* and an emphatic preachment of the fearful penalty that *must* be paid by all who ignore the law. Only thus can we hope to regenerate the race; restoring mankind to health; establishing a higher civilization, and developing a superior race of men.

As an illustration of the virtuous who become victims to the wiles of degenerates, let us take for an example the girl who falls prey to the white slave organization. Admitting at once that she suffers all the tortures of mind and soul so often depicted; is it true that she is entirely blameless, having taken no steps that might lead to her downfall? Apparently some girls are enticed away from home and friends, though others, more beautiful, desirable, and attractive are unmolested. Why is this? Possibly if we seek deep for cause we will find a desire for adventure; that pleasure, jewels, and beautiful clothing, were the lure employed by the exploiters in inducing the girl to forsake all really worth while for an apparently glittering future.

Innately these girls, though good of heart, are unsatisfied with their home life, friends, and the ordinary pleasures the community affords. They look with longing eyes to those other possessions and pleasures of which so much has been written. What is the result? When the flashy, versatile stranger appears, he quickly notes the dissatisfaction and seeks acquaintance; he plays upon the emotions as does the master musician on the harp; he fires the imagination, and promises all in heaven and earth. Admittedly, nearly every one of these girls is honest at heart, but all scruples are readily overcome by the false promise of honorable marriage.

We have indicated the several reasons why it is apparently easy for the exploiters of virtue to find victims—because of the dissatisfaction of these girls with their environments, friends, possession, and pleasure. There is an inborn *cause* for this discontent, and the readiness to form acquaintances with strangers without proper introductions and the consent of parents; basically it is similar to that of the perverted youth.

Parents live a life of prostitution; the mother consents to the husband's request because she desires his support, clothing, luxury, and home. In innumerable cases there is no love between them and the marriage is one of convenience or pleasure, only. On his part, he gives because she demands it, or by reason that he has been taught it is his duty. On her part, she chooses the easier way by selling herself for the comforts it brings her, or mayhap because she wishes to avoid the scandal of a divorce. Whether the fault of one or the other, or both, the fact cannot be gainsaid, the marriage rite is desecrated, and either one or both prostitute a Divine gift for selfish purposes. Prostitution is such whether the indulging pair are legally wedded or not, and ultimately results in children who are not wanted, therefore *unfortunately born;* not in love, consequently *without love for the good and the pure;* naturally dissatisfied and with an insatiable hunger for all that is unattainable in the home environment. *There is no soul, or spiritual desire in the heart for the real, lasting things of life, consequently no resisting force against the wiles of wolves in sheep's clothing.* This is not even the worst feature in these cases; the children conceived in passion, undesired and cursed before birth, never *receive the proper care and correct training.* Who can blame them if they become scarlet women? Our pity, as is God's, should be with them. We maintain: Assuming man and wife love each other, being possessed of a longing for children to bless their homes, having a correct knowledge of the application of creative laws, these becoming parents to a girl under such conditions, and teaching her thoroughly and without sham, though in chaste language, *would never need to fear any white slaver, however seductive his talk and glittering his promises.* Why? Because a girl thus born and instructed would not form acquaintances without informing her parents; nor would she consent to any arrangements without her parents approval. Should such an one be abducted, no force in the universe could induce her to commit, or consent to, wrong; honor being dearer to her than life itself.

Where shall we seek the remedy for these great evils, and by applying it, save the race? Shall we punish the guilty ones, the white slavers and their cohorts, as is the common practice these days, and stop there? This may be commendable, but is hardly sufficient; like all local remedies, it treats the effect, leaving the cause operative. We must remove the cause by fully instructing the present and coming generations the entire *laws of being;* likewise teaching parents all that concerns the procreative organism; by the inculcation of a true knowledge of cause and effect, and the absolute and unrevokable edict that "the Soul that sinneth it shall die," no force in the universe being available to set the law aside or revoke the penalty when deserved.

The girl rightly born and correctly taught will never open the way for anyone to betray her; this is her true salvation and protection; while the boy lovingly conceived and instructed in the laws governing manhood will never entice or degrade womanhood. Meanness and perversions unborn in the heart of boy or girl cannot manifest in their future relationship with their mates.

There is no acceptable excuse for the criminal ignorance pervading humanity concerning the abuses of the generative and regenerative faculties and forces. No longer will we be permitted to plead as an excuse that it is irreligious to instruct our children in these subjects; because of fear they may make unholy use of the knowledge; on the contrary, it is *now become a holy religious duty to instruct the children, clearly and convincingly inculcating the tenet that for the soul to be saved, only divine use (through, and in love) may be made of the creative function, and that to "cast the seed upon the ground," or exchange when lust is the incentive of action, is to damn the body, mind, and finally, the soul itself.*

Every boy and girl able to read will find in any daily paper more degrading information in the scandals voiced, than could possibly be contained in the entire exposition of sex and its laws, when clothed in sane and chaste language. We constantly permit our children to read scandal monging sheets; while consistently refusing to enlighten them respecting the creative functions; nor instructing them in the correct knowledge that they may know how to preserve their honor and purity, guarding themselves against the pitfalls and snares; disease, sorrow, and misery, consequent on the abuse of these functions. Surely we must admit it far more desirable and noble to teach the prevention of wrong than to punish the immorality of which they may be guilty and from which we might have saved them by enlightenment.

Who are those sitting in judgment, issuing edicts that we shall not teach the saving truth? With rare exception it is such as have themselves abused their procreative functions to an extent resulting in impotence; consequently they have knowledge only of the dark, disgusting, degrading aspect; totally ignorant of the elevating, reconstructive, regenerating feature. Another class ready to taboo the entire subject are those of cold, frigid, forbidding temperament, who cannot see aught but wrong in the nature that is warm, sensitive, loving, normal, therefore passionate, *as the great Creator intended.*

The great awakening is due; an enlightenment among mankind generally to the goodness, purity, and nobleness of the exalted creative function; to be utilized for the betterment of man, rather than employed for his degradation; and an appreciation of the fact that if the race is to be redeemed, prompt action is essential, otherwise the fountain of life will become so weakened that cleansing and strengthening will have become utterly impossible.

One reason why many good men and women avoid the light pertaining to sex and its functions, is because for so many centuries they have been deluded with the idea, inculcated by church and state, that the creative organism had no other purpose than procreation and pleasure; and they as yet cannot comprehend the deeper and holier significance and application of the function. They cannot bring themselves to a realization of the uncontradictable fact that any one may be pure in thought or intention who deliberately seeks a frank discussion of the sex question; nor are they as yet awake to the birth of a new age as regards this problem. Whereas, sex has been the means for carnal pleasure first, and procreation last, an incident rather than an intent, for the most part, it is henceforth to become the symbol of the *procreation of desired, longed-for, and welcomed children* and for *regeneration* of *both body and soul, founded upon a basis of mutual love,* and no longer the carnal and degrading act that would shame the lowest brute, not to mention He who created the sexes for holy purposes, and, looking upon his work, saw "that all was good." The sooner mankind can be awakened to a full realization of the new understanding, the earlier we can convince the more intelligent classes among whom honor still exists, the quicker will we be able to start the new race marching onward toward greater achievements, purer lives, and nobler manhood.

The great question confronting us is, where to begin. Undoubtedly the initiative should be with the daughter; and the proper time is the moment she is capable of asking questions, an inquiry clearly indicating thought on a subject which is a mystery to her. We must instruct her, make her understand and *believe* that she is God's most beautiful, noble, and sacred handiwork; that with her is the responsibility of restoring the race to its primitive purity, with an exalted personality. We must explain to her all that concerns herself; why she is woman, for what purpose she is here, how she must guard and protect herself; that above all else she must not permit liberties to be taken; yet remaining normal and natural, a delightful companion, a good partner, and in all affairs demand respect for herself and her creative powers. She must be instructed what are her duties, as well as the rights of man; what she may demand, as well as what may be rightly requested of her, and to what extent she should comply. She must be fully taught the power that resides in her department of creation and how she must employ this in the commencement of the beginning of a superior race. In short, she must come to a thorough comprehension of the glory of her being; likewise an understanding of her weaknesses that she may the better guard herself against the advantages that will be taken because of them.

Let us save the girl by teaching her how to protect herself, never lowering herself for any reason whatsoever. In redeemed and glorified womanhood is the freedom of the race from degradation, savagery, war, and misery. The womb of woman is God's exalted laboratory wherein is fashioned mankind; and when we elevate womanhood, we have given the incentive for the development of a superior race.

One of the great moral cancers eating out the heart of mankind is the almost universal practice of promiscuous sex relationship. Arriving at a period of time when it shall be the exception, rather than the rule, for men to seek carnal intercourse with more than one woman, within a certain time, we will have advanced far toward freeing humanity from the *internal* volcano that is consuming it. The man who has lived a normal life for years, but because of the continued coldness of his wife, forgets the moral code and with favor looks upon another woman, especially the woman for sale, at once fills his blood with a fire no water can quench; if foolish enough to return to his wife and indulge in sexual congress, he will inoculate her with the virus; should children be resultant of the union, they also, will be consumed with an unfilled hunger; is there need to wonder why we so seldom see a normal boy or girl, comprehending that almost the entire world is filled with this unholy fire.

The greatest crime that man can commit against himself and his progeny is to seek sexual embrace with more than one woman within a limited time; yet a greater crime for woman to do so; because she absorbs directly into her bloodstream the various fires which act as would two chemicals not in affinity, when placed in a retort. We wish it distinctly understood that we do not make the statement, or even indicate, that all men are unfaithful to the one woman, whether wife or sweetheart, or that all women are unfaithful, even in thought, to their husbands; we have reference only to that vast army of men and women who find nothing sacred in sex and seek carnal pleasure at the expense of humankind and in defiance of God's fiat.

If it is impossible for a man to arouse the passions of his wife through caresses and other natural means so that compliance to his wishes is willingly granted, he should not even attempt to coerce her, but give her freedom. If unable to control his desires and seeking the embrace of another woman, he must not, under any circumstances, while such relationship continues, have aught to do with his wife; to disobey this law is to follow the Path of Death.

The dire consequences of attempting to harmonize two or more forces by a woman is far more disastrous to herself than it is in man, because the contamination resultant from trying to serve husband and lover is more direct and lasting.

Many moral and honest men, at a moment of forgetfulness allow themselves to be led astray, by friend or passion, thereafter find all their thoughts, opinions and ideas changed; they become discontented with conditions that formerly satisfied them; are unable to learn the cause for dissatisfaction and irritation which may become great enough to part them from the woman they formerly loved. Similarly, the woman who, at a moment of injured pride, pique, or through the intercession of a "good friend," side-steps the straight and narrow path, engenders a fever within herself that destroys peace of heart and mind, and often causes her ultimate fall.

One of the great laws that *must* be obeyed, if health, happiness, and peace is the aim of life, is absolute faithfulness to one mate and perfect purity in the exercise of the creative function. The correct, pure, and holy exercise of this energy is the *key* to race redemption and personal Immortalization; while its abuse is the open door to degeneracy, misery, and war, the Path of Death.

The Great Delusion

All through the ages this ugly monster, continence, has shown its head; and wherever it has trailed its hideous body it has left in its wake the most degraded forms of perversion and degradation. All the crimes in the category of evil follow. The natural use of a part or function produces natural results. The perverted use of an organism or function produces undesirable conditions and destructive consequences. Health, saneness, mental and physical equilibrium, all these blessings are found by those living in harmony with sex laws. We can, *and do,* find the opposites of these blessings among the followers of continence.

Continence

Part One

A Damnable Doctrine—A Doctrine Which Damns

Were it incumbent on me to name the most harmful, destructive, degrading, debasing, corrupting principle taught today by several of the philosophical and religious organizations, I should at once state: "The Doctrine of Continence."

God made no mistake in His creation. To suppose that He instituted a department in life, established laws for its welfare and continuance, and then annulled them, is to impute to the Maker both indecision and lack of knowledge. Everything in nature is balanced—that is, *dual*. A one-sided condition cannot exist.

Man was created by and through the wisdom of the Creator. Male and female created He them, and we may rest assured He made no mistake. His plans for the human race contain no errors and man cannot improve upon the laws given him for his guidance and growth. If God had ordained that the *organs of creation* were to be and remain inactive, would He have created them in the manner they are?

Granted that God created the sexes, the argument is advanced He intended them to be employed solely for the purpose of procreation, that is, the production of young through generation. Such an argument is illogical and unworthy of a sane, sensible mind. Nature is dual, an incontrovertible fact, and her methods of working out the law prove it. God's plan of sex is also dual—dual in form and in purpose. The pendulum swings with equal precision both ways. The opposite of male is female; of generation, re-generation; of procreation, creation, or the *re*-creation of the self-being. Voiced in simplest language: Through sex, by generation, is brought about the propagation of the race, or the creating of life in another body; through sex, by *re*-generation is developed the life "more abundant" in the self-body. Therefore, sex is of as great a necessity to the individual as to the race; and the welfare, growth, and unfoldment of the individual is in exact ratio to the importance of populating the earth. Continence has no status in the Law of Life.

If sex activity is a violation of the Law of God, then all those who disobey that law must suffer the penalty. (We are now dealing with the normal man and woman, not perverts.) It is beyond dispute that men living in harmony with law, reap the benefits of their obedience. For example: Men working in conjunction with the law governing the physical body possess health; those planning and executing in unison with the law of prosperity have wealth and possession and so on *ad infinitum*. *The greater the harmony between God and his children*, the more of good bestowed upon man. If non-use is the law of sex, then the comparatively few unmarried men and women of absolute chastity come under the bounty of the law, being "perfect in the law" they should, and would be, gods and goddesses in greatness of power, beauty of person, and advance in development, not to mention the vivacity and sweetness of disposition. Do facts manifest this? Do the adherents of continence possess these desirable qualifications? Do we not more often find the approach to these characteristics in the happily married of much mutual embrace (so admitted by them), than in the unmarried? Facing fairly without evasion this important question, one must admit that the followers of sex-continence usually exemplify unfortunate traits and most undesirable weaknesses.

To understand so complex and personal a subject, every important phase must be thoroughly investigated.

Many people otherwise intelligent, voice the inane argument that as animals cohabit only for the perpetuation of their specie, men should be satisfied with an imitation of the creatures of the lower order, and abandon the results attained through evolution; in other words, ignore the human development of the mental, physical, and spiritual nature. One might as well argue that the instincts and propensities of the cow or cat should serve as an example to those spiritually awakened, as to liken the demands of animal nature or plant life to those of the evolving and developing human being.

Nature has perfectly adjusted the requirements of the animal and plant kingdoms to the laws of those realms. The line of demarkation between man and beast is distinctly drawn and an equal distinction exists in the laws governing them. Men are supposed to live in harmony with God, which includes all other harmonies. Animals and plants live in conformity with the purposes of nature; whose one great incentive is the reproduction of their specie; resultantly, the exercise of the creative function takes place only when this can be accomplished. Dominated by the law of her being, the female animal consents, and conception occurs, while she is in season. When the lunar period is past, she refuses all advances of the male, fighting if need be to free herself of these attentions. This attitude is in conformity with the laws governing animals and in no way applies to higher beings. Possessing only the lower nature, the animal has no possibilty of re-generation, consequently, there is neither call nor reason for sex activity, except for reproduction.

Human beings are governed by an entirely different law. Woman does not conceive during the lunar season, but just before or shortly after. We do not say that conception does not take place during that period, or that it cannot, *but we maintain it should not*. To conceive during this period is a crime against the Creator of the sexes, the mother who consents or suffers it to occur, and the child to be born under such a condition. The result of conception during the lunar season is always undesirable; an instance of this is the Biblical story of Esau.

There is as much difference in the law governing the demonstration of sex, between the human and the animal, as there is in the matter of clothing or covering, or in the kind and preparation of food. It is not only irrational, but criminal as well, to exalt the animal kingdom as an example for the human.

There are as many reasons against the practice of continence, as there are tones in the musical scale. We state here the most obvious, physical one. It is immaterial what the man's work may be, whether fatiguing bodily labor or nerve-exhausting study; or how gross or spiritual his employment or vocation; how little he thinks or how philosophically, the body is a laboratory continuously refining the seminal fluid and storing it for use. Sooner or later this fluid, more correctly termed an "elixir," must be used or removed.

We employ the words "used" and "removed" advisedly— they express our exact meaning. Take the highest form of life which man is capable of living; the man of superior wisdom, one with a divine understanding of the laws of God, and through this knowledge knows how to use the seminal fluid for the regeneration of his self, his body; even then there will be a surplus and if this is not absorbed in a natural manner, it must be removed from the system in some way; by the urine, or otherwise. If allowed to remain in the body unabsorbed, it becomes stagnant and therefore poisonous to the system; what is more and worse, it has a deleterious effect on the cellular tissue of the brain and the powers of will and discrimination are adversely influenced. This often results in the perversion of the sex function and ends in damnation. Physical and mental health demands that the seminal elixir not used for creative purposes should be turned into other channels—that of regeneration and in renewing life and strength.

The higher the understanding a man has of the qualities and destinies of the human race, the loftier will be his conception of the *powers* and parts of the individual. Conclusions are based on a true foundation when man admits that he was created with a powerful sex nature to be used in wise and holy ways. To limit that use; to confine its action to the purpose of reproduction, is abnormal.

The laws of God and nature do not limit man. The seminal fluid is created in abundance in the system; if a man lived a polygamous life, and in addition consumed all that was needed for the re-creating and renewing of his own body, even then, the secretion of the elixir would exceed the demand.

There are extremists, esthetically speaking, who deplore what to them, appears the commonness of the sex impulse; men and women particularly who emphasize the sordid physical side; are repulsed by it, and declare that procreation is the only excuse for cohabitation. These transform one of the greatest blessings of God into a curse or a calamity; these same people are on a par with a class of parents who are "too nice" to admit the normal birth of children and delude their offspring with the idea that babies come from heaven or the drug store at the instigation of the stork. Such stories may appear more esthetic than the truth, but why try to explain one of God's greatest and most mysterious operations through the medium of a lie?

It is inconsequential what one person or many have to say on the subject. Our assertion that continence is *not* sanctioned by God is the truth and cannot be successfully contradicted. We must accept the laws of God and Nature; we are no longer living in an age of fools and delusionists. It is beyond the ken of the thinking man and woman how any one can argue that *anything in the realm of law and order, God's world,* requires an apology. There is nothing to be ashamed of, nothing that can possibly be hidden. All law, and the action thereof, is noble and beautiful; the old conceptions and feelings of shame must be abandoned; all that God has created is noble, good and holy.

The fiat of God, the laws governing sex life, creation and recreation, cannot be nullified by man. They may be perverted, traduced, or set aside, *but time finally adjusts the equilibrium; right ultimately prevails.* The creative laws of God are mightier than the beliefs, customs, or religious inculcations of His creation.

Institutions, laws and usages, public opinion and Dame Grundy have done their best to dig a pit and bury this important subject of sex. Whether one practiced continence or not was of little moment, so long as it was not discussed. Whether right or wrong, let the advocates of continence teach it if they liked, so long as it was not taught *en masse,* or openly contradicted. Silence and ignorance were considered virtues. The subject will not down. Had it been possible, this method would long since have annihilated it. We can no longer keep silent; *we who know the truth must proclaim it.* The diseases, mental and physical, arising from an adherence to continence, formerly laid to other doors, must now be recognized as the legitimate resultant of a perverted law, and their cure sought.

All through the ages this ugly monster, continence, has shown its head; and wherever it has trailed its hideous body it has left in its wake the most degraded forms of perversion and degradation. All the crimes in the category of evil follow. The natural use of a part or function produces natural results. The perverted use of an organism or function produces undesirable conditions and destructive consequences. Health, saneness, mental and physical equilibrium, all these blessings are found by those living in harmony with sex laws. We can, *and do,* find the opposites of these blessings among the followers of continence.

Why this senseless discrimination against certain parts of the body? The food eaten by man is digested, assimilated, and the residue passed on. The part remaining unassimilated, must be eliminated. This is anything but an esthetic process, but nothing is thought of it; it has always been an open subject; consideration of it never thought degrading.

The creative nature is very like the digestive and eliminative ones. Only because of secrecy is this part of the body considered ignoble and abused. The comparison of the different processes is not inapt; health depends upon secretions being assimilated and the elimination of unused material. Do we stretch a point when we say that the physical law acts in exactly the same way, whether it is a colon to be evacuated or a gland? We think not. In either case, suppression or retention is deleterious. If for any reason the bowel does not perform its functions, we do not hesitate to ask a physician's advice or treatment. There are men and women trained to teach and advise in sex matters. Why consult a doctor about one and ignore the other, the more important one?

Is there much, if any difference in the reason and principle of elimination as manifested by the various organs of the body? Food is received into the stomach and reduced to a form essential for its assimilation and the rebuilding of the bodily structure. It is taken up by the blood, charged in the lungs, and rebuilds bone, muscle, nerve, and flesh. Waste passes out of the system through various avenues of escape, not only through one. The bowels, kidneys, lungs, skin and sex arrangement, all assist nature. Is it sane or reasonable to disqualify any one of these because of an ignorant aversion thereto?

If the bowels refuse to function properly, constipation follows; there is a consequent poisoning of the system, termed "autointoxication,"* or self-poisoning. Disease, ultimately producing death, results, unless we remove the cause so that the intestines again perform their normal work. If a man consciously ignores this physical law, is he not guilty of suicide? God's law is cause and effect; Man refuses to assist the bowels to movement; that is cause. Death is the logical effect. The Creator is not concerned how we circumvent His laws, what methods we employ; the penalty is always the same, unfailingly certain. When we are not in harmony with law, we reap disaster. A man is guilty of suicide whether he swallows poi-

---

* "Autointoxication" is an abused term. Reabsorption of poisonous material should be known as "Toxo-absorption." See "Diet, The Way to Health."

son, shoots himself, or refuses to aid a diseased bowel. Before the great Lawgiver these various infractions bring about the same result; all are equally effectual in bringing about disaster.

If the kidneys do not perform their functions properly, illness results. Bright's disease or some other malady makes it manifest that they are not functioning according to the law governing them. If remedies are not applied, death is certain. If the lungs are not performing their duty, they weaken gradually, tubercular indications appear and death is merely a question of time. The law governing is identical in every part of the eliminative system; all these organs receive a share of the nutriment from the food ingested; it is apportioned to them for the rebuilding and keeping in repair of their particular organism. All that is not used in construction and reconstruction is refuse and *must be thrown out, otherwise it will deteriorate, induce irritation, finally destroy. This is the law.*

The law of elimination applies equally to all the eliminative processes of the body. Out of the amount of nutriment furnished the body the sex organism selects its own portion. It cannot appropriate every particle of it any more than the intestines or kidneys use up their share. In every department of construction and repair there is waste; *this must be taken care of one way or another.* If the unwholesome, insanitary, contrary-to-law idea of continence is followed and the waste retained, it is thrown back into the general system as a positive poison and ultimately induces disease and is the cause of death.

The pathological effect of various infections produce different diseases in the body; that is, the action of poisons secreted by the different organs is resultant of numerous ailments. The effect of a diseased kidney is unlike that of a congested liver; though the disease of the kidneys has a direct influence on the sex organism, because the kidneys are the laboratory wherein the *seminal fluid is produced.* The infection due to stagnant seminal fluid is far-reaching and elusive; the poison thus generated not merely effecting bodily tissues, but through the blood and nervous systems attacks the centers of mental activity. The reasoning faculties and the moral nature succumb to this insidious taint. The imbecile and the pervert are extreme examples; but the world is full of other victims inoculated with mental and physical infection. Onanism, sodomism, and the specialized houses in the red-light districts of the larger cities are proof of this. Can any one doubt the necessity of scientific and philosophical instructions on this subject?

The adherents of continence declare that love is the prevention and the cure of disease, whether of the sex nature or of any other part of the body. The divinity of love *is* a cure, but the man or woman living in disobedience to God and His laws is not in a position to talk of or apply the principles of the higher sphere of love. We enter a protest to such a man or woman using the word love; they do not know its meaning. Love and sex are the dual parts of the emotional nature; there can be no true, lasting love without sex. And what is more: *The strength of a man's love equals the virility of his sex power.*

This statement of fact applies only to the love of men and women, such as is the basis of the happily married couple. The very craving for love and affection from one of the opposite sex is based on the sex nature.

Is it possible for a young man to love a woman, who through bad habits or abuse has deprived himself of "manly strength?" *Emphatically no.* Love, as experienced by incarnated beings cannot be divorced from the alchemy of sex. That young man may be mentally faithful to the woman, but that is not love. Go farther. Is it possible for him to love father, mother, brothers and sisters, in the truest sense of the word? Again we repeat *no.* If he is not an all-round man he is not in possession of the prerogatives of man. Follow this question to the ultimate. Is it possible for him to truly love God? The answer is the same emphatic no. To truly love is to love wholly (holy), with the complete nature in wholeness. The man under discussion is not whole; half of his emotional nature is disabled or ruined, and half a man cannot give a whole man's love to either woman or God.

It is apparent that all the famous men and women who have become great in the world of action and accomplishment were those possessing fully developed, normal sex natures. Proven celibates and eunuchs are not listed among the immortals. If there was ever any misuse of the sex function of the famous men and women it was over-use, never non-use.

It is utterly impossible for a man to be healthy and virile and strong, capable of physical and mental activity along any line of the world's work, who does not attend to the organs of elimination in his own body. Neither is it possible for a man to be healthy in body and mind, full of strength and vivacity, who does not live a natural sex life. The man who is love-starved, system-congested, mind-poisoned has little chance of success or happiness.

The so-called doctrine of continence may be likened to a pool of water surrounded by a wall of masonry. The fresh water pouring into the basin which, when filled, automatically shuts off the inflow. From that time on, only an amount of water equal to the quantity soaking away or evaporating finds its way into the pool. What is the result? A child could guess the answer. *Stagnation*. The life and the purity of the water depends upon an inflow of fresh water which is denied it. All through this liquid body poison generates and each particle seeking an affinity rises to the top, unites itself to other bits of virulent matter and forms a sheet over the water. In and through and underneath this foul blanket are minute, evil creatures and we call it the "poisoned pool."

As every pool of water requires an inflow of fresh water to keep it sweet and wholesome, so does the sex nature or system of man need a constant inflow of the vital fluid. This presupposes an outflow. If the outlet is denied, nature seizes other means of remaining active. Continence is an automatic shut-off, for only an infinitesimal amount of fresh material can find entrance, the organism being already surcharged and overflow-ing with stored-up semen. The result is stagnation. Poison generates in the congested area, unites itself to other poisons and finds its way through the tissues to different parts of the body. This poison is readily taken up by the blood stream and nervous system; and its baneful effect is worse than death. It disturbs the equilibrium of the entire system of man; undermines the moral nature; detracts power from the will; and, through irri-tation, adds impetus to the desires. The natural, normal outlet being closed the action and the purposes of the creative nature turns its force in upon itself. Perversion and a thousand evils spring into being under the foul blanket of continence. The mentality becomes as thoroughly diseased and hopeless as the body of a man who finds himself afflicted with leprosy, and a mental leper can no more think clean, wholesome, healthy thoughts than a poisoned pool can give forth a stream of pure water.

The Fiat of God

It is inconsequential what one person or many have to say on the subject. Our assertion that continence is *not* sanctioned by God is the truth and cannot be successfully contradicted. We must accept the laws of God and Nature; we are no longer living in an age of fools and delusionists. It is beyond the ken of the thinking man and woman how any one can argue that *anything in the realm of law and order, God's world,* requires an apology. There is nothing to be ashamed of, nothing that can possibly be hidden. All law, and the action thereof, is noble and beautiful; the old conceptions and feelings of shame must be abandoned; all that God has created is noble, good and holy.

The fiat of God, the laws governing sex life, creation and recreation, cannot be nullified by man. They may be perverted, traduced, or set aside, *but time finally adjusts the equilibrium; right ultimately prevails.* The creative laws of God are mightier than the beliefs, customs, or religious inculcations of His creation.

Continence

PART TWO

The problem of sex is an individual one like that of dietetics. Men differ from each other; and while different foods and various combinations are required for the several bodies, still the general laws of nutrition apply to the entire race. The laws governing the creative function also have a general application, but the adjustment of each *must be in harmony with the law.*

Elimination of waste material from the physical organism must be thoroughly effected, the amount of matter being in proportion to the quantity of food taken into the system.

Some men store up an immense reserve of vital force. Even though a more than normal amount of this essence is expended in business life, there is a surplus left for elimination; and the normal, natural method of expending this is through the marriage rite. In case of the unmarried, special consideration must be given the subject, though if the food is limited to normal quantities, the thought-world freed of sordid, sensual thought; physical and mental effort followed daily, nature will regulate and eliminate the surplus, either during sleep or through the urine.

That Race Regeneration may obtain, the laws of God and nature must be understood, not merely guessed at. It is inconsequential what opinions have been our guide, if they are contrary to, or out of harmony with, *creative law,* they must be abandoned. *Truth* must be our motto, our *guide. Truth only,* nothing less.

This problem is of individual and national importance. Normal sexual exercise is not only essential to health of mind and body, but equally so for the procreation of a healthy, normal, symmetrically developed race in the future.

It is impossible for any man having indulged in the embrace, to thereafter live the continent life for any length of time, a year or more for instance, then perform the marriage rite with any satisfaction and become the father of a superior child. It is doubtful if he can call into being even a normally healthy one. Mediocre in intelligence and talent it assuredly will be. Why?

The following illustration will answer: If a spring of water is damned up, the outlet shut off, the water becomes stationary, resulting in stagnation. *Life is activity* (circulation). If the water is not continually renewed it becomes poisonous, putrid. No one would think of drinking it in this state; and that it may become cleansed and desirable for use, the correct method would be to drain the water, thoroughly cleanse the well or reservoir, then allowing the fresh water to flow in.

The creative springs of a man's being operate in exactly like manner. If a man dams up the fountain of youth; if through a mistaken conception of the laws of sex life he refuses to keep the seminal fluid in circulation, it remains in the reservoir-like glands, becoming stagnant. The vital force, through repression, and inactivity, loses its highest quality and becomes destructive. To create a healthy being, it is necessary to exercise the reproductive organism; that the life-giving fluid may be potent in its energy. If, after a year of continence, man attempts to call into creation a new being, he may actually be able to do so, but the life forces being in the condition of the stagnant waters, coming from an unclean source, it will be both mentally and physically diseased.

What of the feminine side of the question? In a medical practice extending over many years, in the treatment of thousands of women, we have never found a normal condition where the husband was a victim of the belief in continence. Without exception, the organs of the woman's generative system were diseased. Misplacement of the uterus, inflamed ovaries, ulcerated cervix, with resultant more or less continuous leucorrhoea, were part of her ailments. The practice of continence not only sexually weakens and damns the man, endangers the offspring both physically and mentally, but also curses the wife with untold ills.

The man who persists in this unlawful (Biblically) practice will find a gradual lessening of his general ability; his mind becomes less keen; is unable to analyze minutely; loses the incentive to plan and act, becoming mentally negative. Physically he soon drops below par; shortly nursing headaches, becoming nervous and irritable and acquiring dyspepsia. With the suppression of sex activity appears a general inertia and the development of neurasthenic tendencies.

The undesirable effects outlined are only the beginning of the curses that trail in the wake of this destructive practice. Following the weakness of the mental faculties and the general inertia of the body, is the debilitating influence on the power of reason and will; the disintegrating of the moral stamina. It is only a step in advance of sex perversion. Possibly the most heart-rending confessions to which we are continually forced to listen are those of men, many in their youth, who, through well-meaning intentions or modern Onanistic preachments, have attempted to live the continent life, only to find that when they finally awoke to their duties as husbands, they found themselves so weakened that they were unable to even commence performing their duties. What was the natural consequence? A disillusioned wife either accused him of expending *manly* strength with some other woman, or sought out a lover to replace the weakness displayed by the man who should have loved and *embraced* her.

The sex exercise of man is a natural function. Contrary to the same function and its exhibition in the animal, it is not for procreation, and that alone, but for *the regeneration of the whole man, mental and physical.* The great Creator had this in view when He gave man woman as his daily companion.

To single out conclusive proof (that sexual exercise was not intended for one purpose only) from the mass of contra-

dictory arguments and teachings, is not at all difficult. Con-
trast the inclinations of the human with the animal. In the
lower order, where instinct rules, not thought and the *capacity
to plan,* the female seeks the male (note this law carefully) during her lunar season. At no other time does she indicate mating
desire; nor does the male recognize her existence, as a female,
before or after that period.

Had He who created men and animals established the
identical laws to govern both alike, why did He implant in the
two separate creative instincts respecting the same function?
Why are animal and human instincts radically and fundamentally different? Why is coition during the lunar period
sought by the animal female, and absolutely repugnant to the
human female?

As already noted, the female animal desires cohabitation
during the season of reproduction; the male is attracted to her,
and sought out by her, at this special time. It is radically different with the woman, the opposite in every respect; unclean
during this period, the time of the menstrual flow, she is pas-
sive; normally the idea of embrace repulses her; if caresses
awaken her desires she yet refuses all advances, unless she has
become one of the rapidly increasing number of perverts. Should
she desire conjugal exercise during the time of her uncleanliness,
if it is forced upon her and she conceives, the result is always
a marked child; bearing the stamp of (blood) Cain.

Unlike the animal, except in extraordinary cases, the
woman exhibits affection and desire after, not during, her hours
of abstinence. If she conceives shortly after this period, a
strong child should be the result; and it may be stated in passing, that the greater the passion—love being one of the aspects
of her desire—the stronger and more virile will be the offspring.

The possibility of conception decreases with the passing of
the days following the moon's phase. After ten days there is
little danger of pregnancy occuring; and it is not likely she will
be able to conceive until a day or so before the actual commencement of the next period. Should conception result during

the pre-lunar season, the child is liable to be deficient in vital force; the life-sex-energy stored up in the mother from the previous purification having become depleted and thus prohibiting her from bequeathing the full vitality which she herself does not possess.

There are generally days each month when most women are incapable of conceiving and reproducing her specie; a period wherein she may, nevertheless, greatly desire the conjugal embrace. If the laws of the animal world were given for the guidance of the human race, why was the mother of the race granted fourteen sacred "open days" wherein fasting is not demanded of her? The moment a female animal desires, she seeks satisfaction. If continence is a sound doctrine, why should the female of our specie be filled with unsatisfied longing more than one-half of her time? The fact is, *Revealed* religion has enlightened God's children that during this time man (and woman through him) may contract with the inhabitants of the Stellar spaces, and receive strength and wisdom for his guidance.*

Accepting it for granted that the husband is her equal, can an advocate of continence maintain that the woman does not obtain health, strength, and greater power to love, through the practice of the marriage rite? This assertion of ours, that she *does* derive great benefit, does not apply in its entirety, as when the husband is abnormal, or a weakling. Can the continence devotee deny that, under *harmonious conditions,* the participants of the holy (whole) rite receive spiritual and physical blessings, during these "blessed days of non-fasting?"

It is apparent to all but the ignorant and narrow zealot that God instituted a different creative, and re-creative, law, for man than that of the animal. Men and women *do* find strength, health, and *renewal of youth,* together with all powers and blessings, through obedience to the law of *correct* use. Sexual exercise is a source of incentive in both thought and action; the

---

* Taught at length in the "Arcanum of Sex."

stronger the sex potency the greater the power generated for achievement; it is the source of health, of happiness, and of all that benefits life.

When we speak in this broad, emphatic manner, we have in mind rational indulgence, *not* license. Normal exercise and license are as far apart as the poles of the earth. One induces health and all desirable possessions; the other is an incitant to disease, morbidness, perversions ofttimes, and the destruction of all that is good, ending usually in an ignoble death.

The sensual desire should be controlled in the same manner as all other appetites. A wise man eats only sufficiently to supply the requirements of the physical being. Too much food congests the entire system. Sexual indulgence in excess depletes the nervous system, the very opposite of the effect desired. The exercise of the creative function must be only in so far as it is conducive to health and vitality; a normal satisfaction always resulting in peace and contentment.

The question of temperament is of vast importance in dealing with the issue under consideration. Race Regeneration cannot become a science until individual dispositions, and the combinations, good and bad, of constitutions, are understood. Ignorance of the requirements of different temperaments is productive of sin and suffering; the mating of natures is quite as important a problem as the mating of bodies. For example: A man of vital temperament, full of virility and force, ought never to marry a woman of a cold, unimaginative, plegmatic nature. Such a union will make of existence a hell for both, and children resultant of the union are certain to be deficient along some line of mentality, and most always afflicted with a pronounced bodily weakness.

Temperament is usually indicative of the degree of sex potency in man. Contrary to general opinion, the nervous temperament is not the most passionate; the nerve energy displayed dissipating much of the creative forces. Careful selection of a fitting mate is of prime importance; race development depending upon right selection. A normal child can be expected only when happiness attends the marriage rite and that is impossible where the twain are improperly mated. As abnormal children often result through the mating of virile fathers and cold mothers, so also, do they appear when the mother desires the embrace of the father thrice a week, in harmony with the rules of Solomon, and is reluctantly granted it once a fortnight. Such an instance is in mind: Only a week before the writing of the above, a woman, one whom we had cured from a severe nervous affliction, now the mother of two children, and *en ceinte* with the third, confessed to us that the severe attacks of nervous irritation, amounting to irrational action, as the direct resultant of a continuous hunger for the embrace, this being granted her possibly once a week, or every two weeks, *then only at her own request,* when as a fact, she desired the rite two or three times a week. What will be the result of such a conception? Has any man the right to become a father, who cannot, or will not (as in this case), righteously support the mother-to-be?*

The inculcation of, and obedience to, the doctrine of continence, will never regulate the tendencies of the age, nor succeed in reforming them. Quite the opposite; by the practice of such delusitory instructions the very things we wish to regulate, or annihilate, are certain to become more firmly established. Continence is in itself a form of perversion; only in the rarest instances can a man begin living the continent life without showing signs of weakness, nervousness, and would he confess the truth (many have); mental distortions—the thoughts and imaginings leading to perversion. This is the first stage of deterioration; the second follows close on its heels; love of none, selfishness, finally degradation.

A normal, unsatisfied appetite incites to a perversion of that desire *without a single exception.* Suppression of any natural longing, power or potency has never been a success and never can be. *Nothing dies.* When an attempt is made to suppress

---

* As this page is going to press we are in receipt of a telegram from this lady, informing us she is in the hospital, due to a miscarriage, this occurring without any apparent reason.

or destroy a normal tendency, we merely hold it in check for a limited time until a change has taken place in its activity and then it manifests in a new sphere, in some disguise. There is nothing higher on the physical plane than the normal; if it changes its material form, shape, or design, it is become abnormal. Consequently, if a normal sex power is suppressed it becomes unnatural, the first step on the path to perversion.

Men, practicing continence, have been heard to commend their action by voicing the sentiment that if all men were like them, the red light districts in towns and cities would soon be extinct. This is seemingly true; but infers an untruth. It is *not* the men of normal sex practices that give life and support to vice, but men and boys who have been instructed to suppress, or those in an environment of life where normal action is denied them.

Thousands of men are starved in their love-expression, because of the ignorance of their wives. These women have been taught that sex is degrading; that to acknowledge passion in themselves is a shameful admission. They discourage the sacred relationship, and the husbands, if normal, seek relief and understanding elsewhere—usually among the undesirables of a city's population, because *they have too much respect and manhood to approach a girl or woman to whom they cannot offer honorable marriage in exchange for the favor.*

Such women destroy their own love-nature and turn, what should be a happy home, into a mere lodging house. All because they deem themselves purer and holier than the Creator who made them to love and express it; giving them an organism wonderfully constructed for that purpose, but which they deny and abuse.

There are men and women (some of them may possibly peruse these pages), who pride themselves on being adherents to the doctrine of continence, and why? Because for one reason or another, *they cannot be any other way.* They have expended their inheritance in riotous living. They have lost health, strength, and even desire; of these, God has said: "the soul that sinneth it shall die."

There are narrow-minded, bigoted men and women who, because of some bitter experience in life, have had frozen every particle of heart and soul out of them. They cannot love; all warmth has departed; they have lost all power of conjugal affection. They are often termed "vinegar-faced," and deserve the appellation; but these are to be deeply pitied.

Another class, capable of continence in the accepted meaning of the term, are those victims of religious excitement who haunt revival meetings. These are generally sexually diseased, and while in a state of hysteria, often unknown to themselves. experience the *orgasmal crisis;* leaving them relaxed, weak, but satisfied of their holiness. These same people, usually women, are loudest in their praise of continence, while as a fact, they are the victims of self-satisfaction (unconscious self-abuse) brought about by religious fervor, a condition a thousand times worse than the exercise they deplore in others.

There is a type of men who consider woman of value only because of her capacity to gratify his damnable lusts. These cannot be persuaded that woman has desires and a right to experience the same pleasurable sensations. These brutes are the curse of God's holy creative institution, they exercise the function for themselves only; having completed the act, leave their partner in a state of feverish excitement. God has pity for these victims; they suffer exceedingly for no fault of their own. A continual repetition of this destructive practice is resultant of an internal irritation; inducing in time an abnormal condition of the creative organism; and acting as an incentive to the purest woman living to either indulge in solitary vices or become the mistress of the first *real* male with sense enough to recognize the condition. Were we to be the arbiter in passing judgment on such an one, we would free her with a blessing and imprison the brute guilty of her fall.

Women are not the only sufferers in this respect. There are countless men, affectionate and true of heart and nature, gifted with virile power and purpose, filled with love and honor for their wives, who have every natural request refused. Their sense of honor, and loathing of promiscuity, effectually prevents them from seeking satisfaction outside of their own fireside. Such desire for conjugal affection remaining unsatisfied induces an irritation of the urinary canal, the glands become inflamed and swollen, and is resultant of many pronounced cases of Prostatic ailments; is ruinous to love and affection; so that which was once the basis of honest love and affection, a normal, God-given inclination, is destroyed.

A certain type of women must be blamed for another phase of this evil. There are many good men married to women who refuse the duties of motherhood; who refuse to bear children; yet desire, aye, demand, sexual exercise. They decree he shall be with them for a time, then withdraw. Both are robbed, though the man is ignorant of any wrong-doing. Through disobedience to the great law enunciated by Moses, "Thou shalt *not* cast thy seed upon the ground," disease accrues to both of them; they destroy their very souls; grow to hate each other and home becomes a hell.

Sex exercise must be carried to a conclusion in a perfect manner. There is a right and a wrong way; no man is privileged to embrace a woman unless she expects to obey the sex law which God and nature instituted. The law of reciprocity is *positive;* when the embrace is undertaken the twain must not separate until both participants are fully satisfied. When this fiat is faithfully obeyed, there is no loss of vital force by either of them, he absorbs the magnetic potency contained in her Lochia; she the vitalizing principle, the virile energy, which is the life of the seminal fluid. Thus is life, health, and happiness exchanged between the two.

In our walks up and down the pathway of life we meet all classes; now and then we find a woman who has passed through life without knowing either the benefits or pleasure of the sexual embrace; usually resultant of an unfortunate love-affair; and the bitterness and disappointment of it turns her against love, or any expression of it. Such women are usually rabid in their denunciation of the sex relationship; they condemn everything connected with it. These are proof of our contention that continence affects the mental as well as the physical nature, of its adherents.

To another class belong the poor women whose husbands, while themselves receiving some pleasure and benefit from suffering she, through weakness contribute none in return. The strength of his manhood has already spent itself and he retains none for the supplying of the demands of the home. The divine side of the sex life is a sealed book to the wife of such a man; all that symbolizes him a man, and would develop in her the highest womanhood, is missing. She resents the brutal side, as she well may, and if possessed of the courage, forces her weakling husband to discontinue his advances. These women become advocates of continence; can one rightly blame their attitude?

There are also men who became diseased in early life, later victims of perversions until nothing remains but the husk. These men have never known the embrace of a womanly woman who in her love offers all; such men rant and rave, and voice their belief in continence, to the contempt of all who understand the reason.

We fearlessly make the assertion: *There never was a healthy, normal, rightly-born man who had any inclination to live the continent life.* We except men fired with holy religious zeal.

God said: "While the glory of woman is her hair, the glory of man is in his strength."

God Made no Mistake

God made no mistake in His creation. To suppose that He instituted a department in life, established laws for its welfare and continuance, and then annulled them, is to impute to the Maker both indecision and lack of knowledge. Everything in nature is balanced—that is, *dual*. A one-sided condition cannot exist.

Man was created by and through the wisdom of the Creator. Male and female created He them, and we may rest assured He made no mistake. His plans for the human race contain no errors and man cannot improve upon the laws given him for his guidance and growth. If God had ordained that the *organs of creation* were to be and remain inactive, would He have created them in the manner they are?

Continence

PART THREE

In considering, and refuting, the arguments voiced by the exponents of continence we cannot afford to ignore, or overlook, the opposite side of the question as lived and defended by a class of men whose opinions are just as dangerous to the welfare of society; we have reference to the debauchee and the libertine. One extreme is as deleterious, individually and collectively, as the other.

The class just mentioned consider life worth living only when allowed the privilege of exercising excess; variety and promiscuity appeal to them; is necessary to their happiness. Like the gourmand who lives only to eat, these brute beings exist only for the enjoyment of a sensual life; they are slaves to appetite. The pendulum swings both ways, the extremes are abnormal; on the one hand the libertine; on the other, the continent exponent.

Those who preach and practice continence starve the entire being by refusing to supply it an exchange of vital magnetism; thus gradually poisoning the life stream through stagnation. Those who preach and practice various excesses are poisoning the system with streams of magnetism absorbed from many sources; counter currents one to the other; the different rate of vibration shocking and disintegrating the body of the one guilty of the unholy practice. Disease and death is inevitable. The man who desires to live a sane, safe, natural life, chooses the middle path.

The question frequently asked: "How often should sexual exercise be indulged?" The answer requires delicacy and thought; the frequency depending upon the state of mind and body of the individual; the requirements of the person seeking information, always entering into consideration.

There are well-defined indications of the right use of sex laws which, if observed and followed, will give the correct answer to every questioner. So long as the embrace is exercised by two people who love each other, and a feeling of well-being and joyousness, without a hint of shamefulness, is resultant, it is a clear and unmistakable indication that there has been no overindulgence. When the man feels equal to the day's task and is enabled to do it easily and cheerfully; when the woman finds it a joy and satisfaction to perform her duties, and her labor does not seem in the nature of drudgery, then normality is clearly evidenced. Under such conditions, the act is an incentive.

The man and woman whose present, and future, welfare signifies more to them than the immediate pleasure of indulgence, will regulate their conduct in this respect. The slightest hint of weakness or lassitude should be accepted as a warning; an indication of overindulgence, proving that the frequency of the embrace must be reduced. When good results follow a stated regime, the parties concerned are justified in believing that all is as it should be. In general, young married people should agree to certain rules and regulations governing the exercise and adhere to them. Three times a week is usually a safe and sane rule to abide by.

Many have questioned whether continence is as harmful to the woman as it is to the man. To those who have sought first hand information, the answer is comparatively easy.

The sexual instinct is not widely different in the male and female; though the effects of the gratification varies; and generally the desire for exercise in a woman has its incentive in an entirely different emotion than that of the man. In him it arises from the desire for indulgence, for pleasures sake; this is seldom true of the woman. With her the act is based more on the longing to give pleasure to the one loved; a woman's love nature being finer and purer and involving higher phases of emotion than that of the man.

The difference between the sexes is both physical and emotional. Physically, in the male, glands form a receptacle for a highly vitalized fluid; contains not only the seed of new creations, but likewise acting as an excitant toward sex exercise. It is this fluid which deteriorates and becomes poisonous if not used continually in the regeneration of mind and body, and in elevating sexual embrace. The woman has no such glands, therefore does not secrete a vital fluid of this nature; though we must not overlook the fact that the vaginal glands secrete a lochia, and this becomes destructive if allowed to remain uncirculated; however, this lochia does not act as an excitant, but as a lubricant; the flow commencing freely when the emotions are aroused by one for whom she cares.

These physical differences are evidence that desire in woman is not based on the storing of the fluid acting as an excitant, but, as previously stated, on a nervous excitement called into action through the nearness and caresses of the male. Because of the lack of glands storing a vital essence, continence is not so harmful to the woman as it is to man, nevertheless, a woman practicing continence does not escape all harm. When the nervous system is aroused and the lochia flows freely into the vagina, it is nearly always an indication of the blood congestion of the creative organism; harm results to the entire generative system unless this congestion is reduced through the natural process of sex exercise.

The destructive effects of continence appear much more quickly in man because his nature is easily aroused, and because of the non-discharge of the fluid; this acting as an irritant to the urinary canal and thereby arousing a feeling of antagonism to everything about him, and a morbidity concerning all of life.

Another reason may be stated why continence is of greater harm to the male than to the female. In her, nature has fittingly established a periodic outlet for the cleansing of the entire body, and especially the generative system. The male has no such involuntary relief provided by nature; he must depend entirely upon the absorption of the essence through the circulation, and sexual embrace.

The much mooted question of the intensity of desire; whether the male or the female possesses the greater, cannot be answered at random or *en masse*. The balance between the sexes is preserved; but as far as individuals are concerned, it varies according to the temperament of different people.

In a practice of many years as a physician, and an equally number of years as a confessor, we have had ample opportunity to investigate this question of intensity. From the confessions of many women, we conclude the desire of the female, when thoroughly aroused by *real* love caresses is of an intensity unknown to any male. Her nervous system is infinitely finer and upon the fineness of the nerves depends the power to suffer or enjoy. As a fact, her nervous system may be likened to the strings of the finest Opera Grand, while his more correctly to the old fashioned square piano. Many women patients have declared without hesitation, that the inflammation of the ovaries, congestion of the uterus and the abhorrent flow of *fluor Albus*, directly due to an aroused passion, but unsatisfied desire. This is so universally true, that we have made it a necessary part of finding a correct diagnosis to thoroughly question regarding the habits of the sex life. In seventy-five per cent. of the cases under consideration, the difficulty could be traced to forced, chosen, or partial, non-satisfaction or continence. In the single, relief may be found in a change of the habits of life, local treatments, and soothing applications. In the married a cure is possible—if we can secure an interview with the husband and help him see his error.

Seventy-five per cent. of the sorrows and miseries of women, whether physical, mental, or domestic, can be traced to unnatural sex conditions; while the diseases of the remaining twenty-five per cent. coming under our observation were the result of a variety of causes, all of which might accentuate the sex intensity of the sufferer: Overwork, and the consequent nervousness reacting on the sex system; too rich foods, flooding the system with a superfluity of material, some of which naturally seek an outlet through the creative organism; while in the case of girls, dancing and other exercises with young men, though unconscious on the part of the girls, arouses the passions and emotions and induces disturbances in the generative system.

Without fear of successful contradiction, it may be stated that while generally sex intensity may be equal in both sexes, mere passion is much more prominent in men than in women. Men seek the embrace as a matter of relief and pleasure, while women, as we have mentioned before, become aroused sexually more through their desire to bestow pleasure on the loved one, than through actual physical passion.

Proof of this is readily found. A man becoming aroused, seeks relief even if it throws him into the arms of a woman he would refuse to recognize at any other time; *this has been the basis of the curse of the human family.* A woman would seldom do this; if she cannot be incited emotionally first, she remains cold to advances; this indicating that affection urges the woman to response, passion easily leading the man. There are exceptions to every rule, but we have in mind the vast majority of so-called respectable men and women. This analysis does not apply to the libertine who glories in his betrayals and amours, nor to the woman of Scarlet Lane who seeks existence through the sale of her body.

In discussing the problems of continence, we wish to place every phase of the subject before the student that misunderstanding shall not occur. It is admitted by all thinkers that the most developed of the human race have not yet reached the ultimate of perfection in the understanding of God's Creative Laws; therefore, though our statements may appear radical, even dictatorial, we do not make them final or absolute; we make them in accordance with the finding of vast experience; and suggest the student compare our assertions with his own observation, and "hold fast to that which is true."

When we maintain that abstinence for any great length of time is contrary to both natural and divine law; when not made necessary through absence or illness, there are certain other exceptions to so sweeping a statement, that must have our consideration. These exceptions but point out the truth and value of the governing law.

For example, take a normal, loving, naturally developed woman, one who may be aroused to passion by love caresses. Suppose she chooses one for husband who ultimately proves to be more brute than man, who, understanding nothing, and caring less, for the fineness and sweetness of the wife's nature, crushes her love and affection by the coarseness and brutality of his sex demonstration; sex, to him, spelling gratification, and that only. When he desires the exercise, he recognizes no such law as the desirability and necessity of first arousing her emotion through caresses, but acts the brute from beginning to end. To the nature of such a woman, the rite is a horrible nightmare, and fills her with loathing; naturally, she remains cold and unresponsive. If she conceives through the unnatural act, a hundred chances to one, whether male or female, the child will be cold by nature, utterly devoid of sex proclivities; and when reaching adolescence, will be able to live a continent life; because that part of the emotional and creative nature is undeveloped if not totally missing. Any one thus born and damned with such a constitution, cannot help his indifference to the calls of sex; being incapable of responding to the emotions normal to the race.

Without doubt, many of the teachers of continence accepted as authorities, are conceived and born under these conditions. Their influence is all the more pernicious *because they are true to themselves when they teach this doctrine.* They speak from experience and believe their lack of desire and sex-expression a normal condition, when, as an actual fact, *they are monstrosities,* born of an accursed, because loveless, union.

An instance in mind is that of a patient, woman of thirty years, who with tears of shame, sought of us the meaning of her singular attitude on sex; requested us to explain why she **seemed** so *different from other girls.* She confessed that she could not comprehend her own emotions, or lack of them; that never once had she desired the sexual embrace; had never felt love for any man; and had no comprehension of the terms, "love and affection." Hearing such subjects discussed, she felt bewildered; all belonging to the tender passion being totally beyond her comprehension.

The solution of the enigma was found through the mother. She had never once been aroused to the desire for sex embrace; had never known any satisfaction. All her children were born under these conditions; were all cold of nature, sexually asleep, or dead; *they lacked ambition; were without the incentive to accomplish anything in life.*

The case mentioned above might be traced back to another generation; the mother being cold and unresponsive; it may well be presupposed that her mother before her had become abnormal through abuse or mismating. Such conditions must be rectified and a thorough knowledge of the laws governing sex is the only means through which this can be accomplished. Race regeneration cannot attain any perceptible degree until all individuals are an expression of, *and manifest,* God's laws. When every man and woman is taught the plain truth of a complete life, the reclaiming of the human race will be well on the way. What can be more sorrowful in the sight of an All-Wise Father than to see his children stumbling along in the darkness of ignorance? If man, through lack of fundamental knowledge, cannot know human love in its various aspects, how can he ever come into an understanding of the love of the Giver of all these gifts?

The statement often made that men and women wholly absorbed, mentally, in some vast undertaking, as inventors, scientists, astronomers, or other vocations requiring intense concentration, can practice continence without harm, is true in a sense; this might apply to a few, really great, mental giants of the time. Such people develop along one line, employ only one power of mind, following their particular idea waking and sleeping; all the other potencies being drawn to that point and used in the furtherance of the one object in life. To such persons, continence is possible without harmful after effects; they apply either consciously or unconsciously, one of Nature's greatest laws—that of regeneration and transmutation. The vital forces generated by the creative system are marshalled to the brain and absorbed through mental activity; not a dozen men in a generation are able to do this.

Many of the ablest physicians of the past and present declare that men of this type border on insanity; in fact, that genius is a form of insanity. The mind concentrated, day in and day out, on one thing, is unbalanced, one-sided, and abnormal; while the unexercised powers of sex gradually decrease, and if continence continues, is finally destroyed; the *fountain of youth is dried up, is forever lost.*

Considering everything, are we not justified in claiming that no one, great or small, can practice continence without injury to themselves and others? Even in the case of genius, if the foundation of the love nature is destroyed, is he not that much the poorer? Has he not done humanity a wrong if he has placed himself where it is impossible for him to love, and feel, with the rest of the race? Are we not safe in venturing the remark that the genius could still have given the world the use of his mighty intellect, and yet have kept the roots of his love nature flourishing? The love embrace is not essential often by such a man to prevent the death of the desire; there are many temperaments that store the vital fluid slowly; nature does not demand the same activity in all men.

The problems of domesticity and "the vice of nations" cannot be overlooked. When a wife believes in, and practices, continence, what is the husband to do? Because the woman chooses, what he honestly believes is the Path of Death, is that a sufficient reason for him to be forced to commit slow suicide? Many husbands, men of honor and decency, are refused "their natural right;" because of the coldness, religious scruples, or continence; some of these men have denied themselves until nature could bear the pressure no longer. Which is worse, disease, insanity, perversion, or the seeking of a mistress? The method pursued in the latter, is at least the normal, natural way out of the dilemma, even though the mistress receives the love and passion forfeited by the wife.

Cases! Their number is legion. Who is to blame? Who shall judge such men guilty of adultery? What is adultery? When is unlegalized indulgence adultery? Why did God give men desire, passion, love, and all the possibilities of growth and happiness and then shut the door to all fulfillment? He *never did.* He did not bestow upon men all the blessings of temperament and then say: *"Thou shalt not."* If the embrace of the woman who is his wife is denied him, *other than because of illness or an unpreventable cause,* if his health, saneness, ability, and happiness depends upon what the wife refuses, who shall say that morality demands that husband to make the renunciation? If he can find another woman willing to be his *helpmate,* who shall say him nay?

This is dangerous ground, even for discussion. It borders on free-love, *a doctrine we are utterly opposed to with all the force of our being.* Free-love, promiscuity, and license, has nothing to do with the Laws of God and the right use of the creative function, *absolutely nothing.* But all sides of the problem—use, non-use, and abuse—all must be faced squarely and a solution found.

We are not giving consideration to the moral leper who is unsatisfied with the wife who gives him the full benefit of her love; continually seeking other women and excessive exercise. We have in mind only the man of honor, not the libertine; the man who learns through experience that sex exercise is necessary for the preservation of health and well-being, not the debauchee whose creed is license.

What is to be done? *There exists a remedy for every evil;* the solution of this difficulty should be effected without delay; not only for the sake of the suffering, unhappy men and women, but for that of the children being born of such unions and lacking the opportunity to develop normally.

Every state should have laws providing for, and covering, these cases. When the evidence is conclusive that the husband, or wife, fails, *through choice,* in conjugal duty; when it is proven that either one or the other refuses to fulfill the marriage contract as generally understood, divorce should speedily be granted; an unconditional decree offered the one who has sought, and been refused, the rights of sexual embrace for a period of six months. An appeal to statuary law ought to adjust and correct the violation of sex laws.

To recapitulate: The right use of sex is important, not alone to the man and woman, but to the world at large. If man lives a continent life for any length of time, the pool of creative energy becomes stagnant and poisonous, effecting health and mental attitude. Children born under such conditions will often be abnormal in one or more respects and therefore a curse to society; an obstruction to progress through conferring the undesirable traits on their progeny, thus perpetuating the evil.

In the face of the category who can say that continence is not a dangerous experiment. It results in harm to every person subscribing to, and actually living it, according to the temperament of the person concerned. Non-use of sex-energy, like the non-use of every other power, destroys the potency and is therefore a direct violation of the laws of God and mother Nature. Continence, whether voluntary or enforced upon us by others, is a crime against God and man.

Continence

PART FOUR

The pernicious effects resulting from continency have already been pointed out as: A gradual drying up of the vital forces, and an inertness and deadening of the organs whose duty it is to secrete the fluid containing the seed, the germs of physical life.

The practice aims straight at the very foundation of life. We are not advancing these arguments as a philosophical dissertation on the regeneration of life, although it would be unfair to evade this side of the question, for while generation is the beginning of all life, regeneration or immortalization is the end of it, "that for which the first was made." The seed, and the means of generation, is also the medium of regeneration. For this reason Moses taught the children of Israel (God's chosen children of *all* races) that if the seed were cast upon the ground it would become a serpent (destructive to the Soul of man), bring death to whoever committed the sin. Under the Mosaic law it was considered so great a crime, that those guilty of it were judged as having destroyed their soul.

There is very little difference in the effect upon man, both body and soul (what the church terms the spirit), whether the seed is cast upon the ground by the unfinished sexual embrace, the practice of solitary vices, or allowed to die in the generative organism; it is destruction of the living seed without performing any useful service, in either case, and the penalty is exactly the same in all three instances.

It may logically be questioned whether the seed is not lost when used for any other purpose than procreation of the race. Emphatically not in the normal relationship between man and woman. In the exercise when offspring does not result, the forces are used in the process of regeneration; there is an equal exchange between the two; he, through the volatile forces in the seed and the vehicle which contains it, gives her health, strength and vitality; she, through the Lochia, bequeaths the same to him. This exchange is absolutely necessary both to man and woman if health and well-being is sought.

Many wives refuse to allow their husbands to complete the marriage rite through fear of pregnancy; these women quickly become haggard and old in appearance long before their time; nervous wrecks after a few years of marriage; neighbors smile and hint at overindulgence. The repeated interruption of the Rite induces an increased desire so that there may be a possibility of the conjugal relationship being abused, but the reason for the personal appearance is not a waste of seed but from the irritation resultant from abuse of the function and *retention* of seed, and the congestion following non-relief. Another great evil due to the crime (crime it is): The irritation in the male as a result of retained seed and congestion, is an incentive for him to seek relief elsewhere than in the home, or shunning that, excessive drinking and other debauchery. Neither husband or wife can profit through the unholy practice; they both lose much when they allow themselves to be aroused and then refrain from gratifying the extreme of desire.

It is declared by those lacking in wisdom, that continence is the law of life—that the sexual embrace used for another purpose than generation, causes an infinite number of life-giving cells to die, or to be wasted. This is absurd. Out of more than a million seed contained in a single ejection of semen, but one spermatozoon impregnates and fecundates the ovum; the rest freed at the time offer their lives on the altar of service—giving an increased vitality to the one germ fortunate to impregnate.

Many of those who inculcate the doctrine of continence attempt to base their delusions on a Biblical foundation, making them all the more dangerous and acceptable by a class of men and women seeking to avoid their duties. Of this class is a sheet before us, issued under the guise of "liveable Christianity," edited in Chicago, under date of October, 1920. The author effuses thus:

"It is indulgence in the sensations of the flesh that disorganize the finer forces of the consciousness. Fleshly desires, expressed or yearning to be expressed, kill out the connection with the spiritual nature within, and turns the body, which should show forth the loveliness of God-Mind, into a charnel house of disease and discord. All attempts to satisfy one's desires, whatever be their nature, through outside alliance gives the lie to the truth that man is complete in himself, satisfied from God, and ultimately leads to dissatisfaction, woe, and death. Can we wonder that Paul, writing of the immortality of the body brought to light by Jesus Christ, exultantly exclaimed, "Death is swallowed up in victory." There is no victory for either God or man so long as man lives in self-imposed slavery to sense, and then passes to the grave.

With such teachings before a gullible people, can we wonder that immorality increases with leaps and bounds; that it is becoming a living nightmare to the man and woman who would seek the Regeneration of the race? All this is in the name of Christ, supposed son of the Father who in His first creation, cast forth the fiat:

"Be thou fruitful and replenish the earth."

We maintain that anyone attempting to follow such instructions will live to drink the dregs of degradation. No living human being can at once damn up a fountain of life and keep the waters constructive. It is physically, mentally, and spiritually impossible; ending in death of body and soul, a return of the Spirit to the Father.

At this moment we have in mind a case of which the closing chapter was but lately written. It is of a maiden lady who had instilled in mind and soul the undesirability of sex expression, aye, even the shame of possession of such a degrading organism.

The lady in question had lived an absolutely virtuous and

continent life until at the age of thirty-eight she was married
to a man in full possession of his strength, and but a few years
her senior.

Through endearments she became awakened to the falsity
of her earlier instructions and a desire to reciprocate affection,
but what was her horror to find that all her forces were locked
up as thoroughly as though they had never actually been
in her possession and that try as she would, everything seemed
to cry out in agony: "Thus far and no farther canst thou go."
Attempt after attempt was made to unlock the flood gates and
find relief, but with no success, and eventually the nervous
system itself seemed shattered. Broken in health, courage, and
spirit, the lady was referred to us, and after a period of suffering and labor for more than three years, she feels that at
last she is approaching normality and is commencing to once
again enjoy life and in possession of a sane outlook which had
been almost utterly destroyed.

We have outlined some of the more extreme results of the
continent life as we have found them in our years of service;
there are many lesser evils which ought to be of sufficient warning to reasonable, rationable, human beings. The first indication of trouble is nervousness in any one of its various forms,
and apparently without cause, then in rapid succession, an irritability making the person a most undesirable companion;
gloominess, a tendency to see the dark side of everything; loss of
appetite and a starved appearance; incapacity to concentrate;
lack of decision and stick-to-it-ness; desire for constant change;
nervous headaches due to a deranged nervous system, and the
inability to digest the food; constipation and toxo-absorption;
ending in neurasthenia, the door next to insanity.

The debauchee's life is resultant of about the same general weaknesses; the wasting of the life forces will deplete the
man faster than he can accumulate; and the mixture of different rates of vibration; various currents of magnetic forces
coming from many women, will destroy the strongest man; de-
magnetizing him, and shattering the life forces.

Continence is a dragon with an hundred heads; each one carrying death.

In many instances the devotee of continence experiences just the opposite of the torrefaction—drying up—of the vivifying forces; there may be an unnatural accumulation; this, together with a lesion of the generative organism, inducing continuous nocturnal emissions; leading to pronounced spermatorrhea and loss of manhood with the consequent depletion of the entire nervous system. No need to write of the wrecks brought about through this process of degeneration, for nearly every one is personally familiar with such cases and their deplorable effects.

One of the most hideous evils following in the wake of continence is masturbation; one of the most destructive and degrading habits of the present human race. The possibility of the continent man or woman to perversion is greater than most people imagine; the temptation being so insidious that it has been succumbed to before the victim is aware of the danger.

We cannot find an argument in favor of the destructive practice of continence. Admittedly there are periods in the lives of most men when it is both right and expedient to abstain from the sexual embrace; as when the wife is ill, or during the absence of either one or the other from the home; but this is merely abstinence, not continence; and the mind does not dwell on the enforced denial; rather looks cheerfully forward to the resumption of the natural love tie.

What of the effects of continence on the happiness of the home?

Those harmoniously mated best bear the strain and stress of married life who practice the marriage rite naturally and normally. Normally here infers that the couple are agreed, not only in regard to time, but likewise in desire. In some instances this may be but once a week, or once in two weeks; in the majority of cases it has reference to two or three embraces regularly every week except during the period of the wife's unholiness.

A husband should indicate his desires by additional caresses and affection; and only when he has aroused in her similar desires may the Rite be performed. No man should touch a woman until she has indicated a preference; under these conditions health, peace, and happiness are naturally resultant of the embrace. If a man brutally ignores a woman's feelings and forces his attentions upon her, it becomes a crime to cohabit; it is married prostitution, ignoble license.

The confession of every human being, could it be secured, would undoubtedly be this: In every case, without one exception, where man and woman are agreed in time and desire they have parted more in love and harmony with each other after the performance of the rite, than before.

Countless men and women can tell of the woes and miseries of being mismated. The husband, lacking in manly strength, leaving the wife unsatisfied; or the wife, fearing pregnancy, refuses embrace, or half-heartedly submits; and so on *Ad infinitum*. In most instances, the ultimate result is unhappiness, illness, mutual distrust, a gradual cooling of the affections; the husband finally seeking a mistress; the wife a lover; or divorce.

Teachers of continence may assert that the diseases and effects here attributed to continence are as easily applied to those indulging in the marriage rite. We have already admitted all this. The penalty for abuse of sex, in or out of wedlock, is equally as severe as for the practice of unnecessary continence.

In other respects the proof may be declared absolute. For example: The long sex life of the man who practices the marriage rite normally; while the continent man cannot claim longevity of sex. Admittedly, if the latter is consistent, he does not seek continued virility. The argument favors the potency of sex; *the man being considered as youthful, or in his prime only so long as he retains his virility.* Thereafter, he is an "old man."

One point remains undisputed. Neither man or woman has any right to practice the marriage rite without love as the impetus. If the act is performed under any other thought, desire, or incentive, it is a violation; and a marriage ceremony, irrespective of who may have performed it, cannot set aside the great fiat flung into space by God.

If husband and wife do not have any real affection, do not love each other, and he demands conjugal "rights" which she grants, they are both guilty of prostitution. The woman will not, *cannot*, release the magnetic fluid and the man is impotent to infuse the vital forces. The crisis occurs; there is a sort of physical satisfaction, but neither receives the psychic, or spiritualized essence which should always be resultant of cohabitation; *the one thing essential to health, strength, peace, and happiness to both.* Writers and instructors have emphasized the act in itself, or the elimination of it altogether, missing the important point just annunciated; though this *must* be the underlying fundamental insisted upon in Race Regeneration. Until this is fully understood and practiced, misery and weakness will continue to be the "benefit" of the marriage rite.

Much comment has been voiced upon the love starvation of the race. *Love is, and always has been.* It is as natural to every human being as breath or food. The advocates of continence would have us believe that we may love without passion. *That is utterly impossible.* The moment a man dearly and sincerely loves a woman, one of the expressions of that emotion is certain to be in sex.

God created man in His own image; that is, He conferred upon man wisdom and love, the attributes of Himself. The fact that man manifests in the material while God in the spiritual, is nowise a contradiction. Men are co-workers with the Great Creator, and the creative, generative organism, together with the *inherent desire to function through them,* substantiates this assertion.

Had it been ordained that men and women should live separately as sex weaklings would have us believe, God never would have implanted in man so generously the incentive to creative expression; nor would He have instilled in man the urge for weekly companionship, ending in embrace, with the beloved, had He intended the indulgence to occur once a year, or once in two years, then only for the purpose of reproduction.

Were it true that man is capable of loving without passion, then the opposite is equally true; men can, and should, perform the creative act without love. Such a thought is revolting; the consequences even more so; it is beastly, certainly damnable.

Love lies at the basis of passion; and in its correct understanding, *passion is the basis of love.* The power in man to love, or hate, or achieve, is in direct ratio to the virility of his creative potency. The weakly sexed, cannot surely love. Therefore:

The man living the continent life is incapable of expressing love in its highest aspect.

The Great Madness

Mrs. Catt Brands as Slackers All Who Fail to Vote

"Women who, now they have been given freedom, refuse to vote, choosing to be subjects rather than sovereigns, are not proper citizens. They are political slackers.

"Men and women who do not vote, though able and capable of doing so, are in the same category as the German people were under Kaiser Wilhelm."—*"The Evening Bulletin," August 27, 1920, quoting Mrs. Carrie Chapman Catt.*

We are heartily in favor of woman suffrage, but we wish to go on record as emphatically denouncing such statements, irrespective of who voices them.

The right to vote has not given women more freedom; nor has it made her any nobler, any more than franchise has enabled to make gentlemen out of thugs. The *true* woman, the enlightened *mother,* has always been free, and appreciated her power, influence and position in society. Moreover, it is the woman who has the deepest respect for her sex who cares least for the vote; fully grasping the fact that she has the power to induce her husband to vote as seems best for the race. We do not claim she will not vote, she may possibly do so, but only because she believes that thereby she is accomplishing good.

It is reprehensible for any one, man or woman, to voice the sentiment that any woman who fails to vote is in the same class as were the German people. Such statements will do more than any other influence to disgust the real womanhood of America.

"History repeats itself!" The backers of the "Interchurch World Movement" also told us, in display advertisements, that any one not supporting that movement could not be considered a *true* American. The Interchurch World Movement is dead beyond resurrection.

We repeat: We believe it justice to give woman the vote, but women's franchise will never right the wrongs of the world; she is just as susceptible to personal influence and graft as the men, if not more so; while accusing the true woman of being Germanized because *she is a better wife and mother than politician,* will embitter her against unworthly accusers and all they represent.

The Spiritual Significance of Sex

For the past seventy-two years (since 1858) there has been established and laboring in America a Society* having as one of its fundamental principles the inculcation of a livable philosophy dealing with the spiritual significance of sex. This laudable Order has been instructing its members in the tenet that God created man and woman so that there might be the procreation of a race; likewise conferring upon them the power to continually employ the creative potency in the Re-generation of their own self-being, thereby immortalizing themselves; thus entering the Eternal realms while yet in the flesh.

The doctrine preaching the Immortalization of the soul of man (soul being usually termed the Spirit) through a correct exercise of the sex function, has been almost universally denied. The general conception obtaining that sex had no province except procreation of the specie; or if unwisely exercised, resulting in death of the body and damnation of the soul; denying the laws of logic which teach us that the pendulum of the clock swinging to one side must likewise swing to the other, maintaining equilibrium.

If it is possible to abuse the creative function to the extent of damnation, then it assuredly is sane to believe that its right exercise has great power to elevate the soul above the carnal, saving it from perdition. Creation is the act of man which calls into existence a new body; *Re*-creation, or *Re*-generation, is the

---

* See "Philosophy of Fire," published by the Philosophical Publishing Co., Quakertown, Pa.

method of transmuting the mortal into the Immortal. Possibly it were better to make a distinction of terms, and say that Re-creation is the process of purifying and strengthening the body that sickness and weakness be eradicated; while Re-generation is that greater work of bringing into manifestation the mighty Soul counter-part of God in man which generally is allowed to lie dormant; returning, at the death of the physical, to the Father in no more spiritualized essence than it left Him when it took up its habitation in the mortal frame.

To the majority of thinkers it appears incomprehensible that the established religious denomination defend the accep-tation of Biblical writings in their literal sense, giving God credit for all Wisdom, while at the same time denying that sex has any other functon than the creation of bodies for souls (spirits) to inhabit, despite the fact that Moses, the great law-giver, based the *salvation of the Israelites during their sojourns in the wilderness on the uplifted serpent.* Interpreted: *On the purification and elevation of the creative energy and the exalt-ing of sex practices.*

The Israelites while on their long journey to the Promised Land, through their ignorance of the Divine Law governing the creative function, so greatly abused, degraded, and exercised it for self-gratification, became such perverts that there was im-mediate danger of the race destroying itself. Moses sensing the impending evil had the wisdom, obtained through his long years of novitiate in the Priesthood, to know that the evil was based on a misapprehension of the right exercise of the function. That a power potent to destroy was equally effective to save. To protect the remnant of the people, he inculcated the *practice,* through the symbology of the *uplifted serpent,* of employing the sex organism for no other purpose than to create new units for incarnating souls, and the Regeneration of the self-being. This he commanded as a *religious rite* ordained by the *living* God and thus he saved the children in the wilderness.

Moses was impelled to impress them with the constructive law, teaching them that the misuse and perversion of the Creative function, and the continued "casting of the seed upon the ground," so terming the "unfinished" as well as solitary acts, would result, not only in the extinction of "God's anointed," but of every people guilty of the unholy practice; that it was equally dynamic in the destruction of the Soul; voicing the fiat that "the Soul that sinneth it shall die," because the casting of the germ of life (seed in the seminal fluid) upon the ground is *soul destroying;* by reason of the indisputable fact that the essence which the laboratory in the kidneys use in the manufacture of "seed" is identical with both nerve and brain material; a misuse of one being abuse of the other.

In the Ancient Egyptian Mystic Religion, in the days before the established Priesthood had become degraded, one of the fundamental tenets, the first lesson to be learned in the Secret Doctrine, was the right use of sex, *i. e.* for the procreation of new bodies, the Recreation of the self-body, and the Regeneration of the Soul within. Moses had been thoroughly instructed in these while a novitiate in the Priesthood; basing his entire moral code on these, and thereby actually saved his followers.

Christianity (established orthodoxy) following the Mosaic dispensation, has continued consistently to refuse the Spiritual side of the moral code formulated by Moses, and by reason of this, it has thus far been practically impossible to interest any major portion of humanity in the great problem which we maintain is basic of the social diseases and degradation on the one hand, and the salvation of *both* body and soul, on the other.

Churchism gives prominence to the doctrine that all children are born in sin, while *revealed* religion harmonizing with Holy Scripture teaches us that though children may be born through sin, that is, through cohabitation by those who lust or do not love each other, nevertheless, they are not born in sin, nor do they actually commit sin before the age of responsibility—*after* the period of change from boyhood to manhood, or girlhood to womanhood. The original sin being resultant of the awakening, and the misuse, of the creative function; all other sins following thereafter. In the Garden of Eden, the first children remained innocent, and committed no evil, until *after* adolescence, when they disobeyed the creative law and indulged in the sexual embrace for pleasure and satisfaction, instead of only for Procreation and Recreation.

Irrespective of all that we have been taught, the creative function may be exercised without sin attached. Had our first parents obeyed God's law, embraced only for the purpose of procreation, or the Recreation of themselves and the Regeneration of their own Souls, bringing them into a likeness of the Father, there would have been no sin, sorrow, or death; but very early after the time of attaining the age of responsibility they learned of the possibility of obtaining pleasure and satisfaction through the act, and in self-seeking forgot God's fiat, with sin as the result, though it must not be understood that pleasure and satisfaction is forbidden man, merely that it *must not be the primary incentive of action;* as a resultant of constructive desire it is permissible.

Accepting the foregoing statements as a correct interpretation of the Divine Law, the reader might conclude there could be no sin provided the marriage rite was completed; and, the woman participating being virile, a child resultant of the union. This is far from a correct or complete statement of the fact; sin being defined as an "act potent of bringing harm to the self, or sorrow and suffering to another." As a fact, a drunkard or a degenerate might be party to an embrace, the union completed and the consequence a child; yet, because of the status of the actors, it might possibly be either a weakling or an idiot. This would confer upon the child an inheritance of sorrow and suffering, consequently be evil.

Likewise is there the possibility of a libertine cohabiting with a denizen of the brothel, flinging into space a new body. The exercise itself may have been normal and natural; but the actors living a degrading life, the new being could hardly be such as God could smile upon; therefore, a creature of sin, possibly soulless and with destructive tendencies.

If those who consider these statements founded on illusion, instead of, as we maintain, based on Divine Law, will give a careful study to the first two books of the Bible, having in mind at the same time, the moral code formulated by Moses, their opinions will undoubtedly greatly change and be more harmonious with the laws of God and Nature governing the Creative and Re-creative functions.

The late war, fearful as it has been, proved to be a potentious awakener. Physicians and thinkers who formerly scorned the idea of sex having any Spiritual significance, now frankly admit our contention. Through this new conception to the potentialities of sex life, it is become possible to teach men and women, boys and girls, the constructive use of the creative function, as also *its spiritual significance*. This but partly accomplished will save more souls within the next fifty years than the total casualties of the entire war; and who shall say that the Universal Constructive Energy, call it God if you will, has not used the cruelty and hatred of men, and their desire to destroy, as a medium with which to enlighten the minds of men, thus giving an incentive to the creation of a Superior Race.

We have previously implied the possibility of the Israelites committing sex sins through ignorance. We still maintain this to be true; the Israelites were "God's chosen people," they believed His statement of the location of a Promised Land; had the faith in His promise to give up homes and renounce many ties dear to the hearts of men. Considering their self-denials and renunciations, it is illogical to believe they would knowingly deliberately do ought which would destroy the possibilities even, of the promised inheritance; yet this is just what they were gradually accomplishing through their destructive practices, and it is written that of those who left Egypt in great faith of soon reaching a haven of liberty, very few lived to see the glorious day; others having actually destroyed body and soul by bringing upon themselves loathsome diseases, through their perverted sex practices.

Ignorance of the laws governing sex and all that pertains

to the creative function is scarcely less today than in the time
when Moses formulated the moral code; and we seriously question whether the sorrows, sufferings, miseries, and ignoble
deaths are not even greater in proportion, than they were in those
ancient days.   In proof of this assertion, we offer extracts from
a letter recently received from one who applied to the bureau
for information.   It clearly illustrates the ignorance of countless mothers:

"In reading your article on the sex relation, one might get
the idea that every sex impulse between husband and wife
should be indulged, or else there will be sex perversion—and I
don't know exactly what you mean by perversion, *so meagre is
the knowledge of the average married couple in the matter of
sex that they have to learn only through experience, and too
often through their mistakes.*"   (Italics are ours.)

This woman, wife and mother, frankly admits she possesses
no knowledge of sex and its functions; and is even ignorant of
any source where she might obtain an understanding; being
forced to learn through bitter experience.   She is a member of
the established church, but has not been instructed in the most
sacred and important functions of her being; does not comprehend the laws which, rightly understood, and correctly lived,
bring health, happiness, contentment, and finally, *Salvation of
Soul,* or as usually taught *eternal life in the heavens above.*

Her comprehension of the laws we teach is incorrect.   We
do not maintain, nor do we inculcate the doctrine that the marriage rite should be freely indulged.   We do assert there should
be a complete and harmonious understanding between husband
and wife regarding the Sacred relation; and that the continent
life is destructive to the happiness of the home, because where
this doctrine is consistently lived, husband and wife grow
apart and disrupt the family ties.

We maintain the absolute law that a husband has no right,
moral or spiritual, to demand compliance with his wishes; being privileged to accept only that freely granted.   To take by
force that which has not been won and offered with love, is

the beginning of disease in her and death to him. Unquestionably this universal practice of legalized rape is one of the worst forms of prostitution, more horrible in its effects upon man than if he frequented the brothel; where his desires would be satisfied with more or less alacrity.

Furthermore, we persistently assert that if two people live together, the husband of an affectionate, loving nature, possessing the virility which designates him a *real man,* and if his normal desires remain continually unsatisfied, either one or two things occur; he proves unfaithful to his vows of marriage, or ultimately practices perversions.

We freely admit there may be reasons for a continent life; as for instance, where one or both parties are under great mental strain, nervous tension, or some severe sorrow. Where one or both of those concerned is of a cold and unloving disposition, divorce, rather than continence, is the solution of the problem, though in some cases this better remedy is undesirable because of children in the family. In the article commented on, we had reference only to the married; the unmarried must be given special consideration.

When many such letters are received, each with an appeal for knowledge, do we not naturally conclude that the demand for correct and rational instructions on Sex Hygiene, Eugenics, Race Development and Regeneration, is acute? It is actually appalling when we once comprehend the necessity for such knowledge and investigate what passes for information on the solution of the problem.

If we desire to enlighten mankind, saving our great nation from the sex perversions such as have destroyed all of the mighty civilizations of the past, including Egypt, Greece, and Rome among the victims, degradations such as sway Europe at the present moment, we must seek the root of the trouble, and there apply the remedy; this we cannot do unless we face the evil without fear.

Unless we are biased, we will be perfectly willing to carefully study all that is written by the great leaders of the Israelites. He did not complain when God gave him the laws governing the creative functions, and learned they were identical with those conferring Immortality on man.

The preachments of all denominations lay great stress on the evils of fornication, adultery, and husbanding the harlot; and rightly so; but nothing whatever is taught respecting the dire results of indulgence of the marriage rite by those who, though married, do not love each other. Pious eyes are closed to multitudes of instances where women are forced to acquiesce to the demands of their wedded partners even though every fibre of their being revolts at the mere request; while an unbelievable number of husbands demand and receive favors of wives for whom they have no love, because they fear accusation of unfaithfulness, though as a matter of fact, the wives granting the privilege of the exercise care no more for their husbands.

We contend now as always, that the husband demanding favors from the woman when she does not love him or is unwilling to comply, will thereby establish in her system disease, and give impetus to a gradual decay of her vital forces; while for him it will mean damnation generally to body and soul if the practice is continued. If children are the issue of such embraces, they will usually belong to the class of moral weaklings, if not actually idiotic. If a boy, he may become a libertine or pervert; while a girl will possibly be another candidate for street walker, whom all condemn; even those who take advantage of her services. Neither boy nor girl is held responsible under the Eternal law, but the fathers and mothers guilty of procreation when love was not the basis of the union.

In countless instances of legalized prostitution, unnumbered children are born; lacking in their love nature, in spirituality, in all that is essential to manhood or womanhood; *all due to being conceived when the incentive to the indulgence was downright lust on the one hand; hatred and aversion on the other.* Such children may be, and often are, the beginning of a long line of descendants deficient in their moral, human, spiritual and divine nature.

How repulsive these statements appear! They are truths nevertheless and cannot be avoided any longer. If we are sincere in our expressed purpose to free this fair earth of prostitution we dare not rest content with our effort to reform the denizens of the unhallowed districts, *but we must cease the procreation of others who take their place;* and this is impossible until we are *willing to consider the act of creation as truly a religious rite, as that of prayer, i. e. a performance of love and devotion,* not as a Black, or Witch's Sabbath, to be shunned in the light of day, and a subject of jest and debauchery by night when darkness enshrouds the earth.

After beginning the inculcation of truths relative to all concerning sex, why not accept squarely the two Divine Commands, which obeyed, would abolish all crime, abuse, and degradation of the creative functions; making of man the superior being he should be, in place of the weakling; the hateful, lustful, and revengeful creature, the instigator of war and carnage, he has heretofore been. "Cast not thy seed upon the ground," and the expressed penalty "The Soul that sinneth it shall surely die," once thoroughly understood and religiously indoctrinated in all preachments would at least quickly help to modify present destructive conditions.

According to all the great law-givers, irrespective of the age, there are but two functions of sex: First, the creation of new bodies through which God must be glorified. Second, (the spiritual function) whereby through the marriage rite the nature of man and woman, the two participating, shall be raised toward God as in the performance of prayer. In both instances the relationship must be based on love and mutual desire; the compliance of the woman won, not obtained through brute force.

If there is to be a reformation in the sphere of procreation, we must begin with the young; teaching them these mighty truths, so they, in due time, will elevate the creative function;

calling into manifestation no children unless they are the personification of love; refusing to prostitute their creative energy, or reproducing their kind through lust.

By commencing to instruct the boy yet in his youth, that the creative function is basically religious, encircles in love and truth just as is prayer and all other worship of God, and continuing the inculcation until he reaches the age of responsibility; by further instilling into his mind that the greatest curse under which mankind has bowed for ages and suffered, is man's inhumaneness in demanding and accepting favors from a woman he does not love; that the only motive permitting sexual congress is love and a desire for the Immortalization of the Soul of both parties; there need be no fear that he will prostitute his creative potencies; little danger of his contracting any of the loathsome and degrading diseases now so prevalent.

We admit that many of those born in lust and therefore the children of passion, will continue in the way of their fathers; but we have in mind a new and correctly born race, a generation of Superior beings, born in love and where wanted.

The boy born in holy (not prostituted) wedlock, who has been instructed in the law, will no more think of seeking the embrace of a prostitute than he would of insulting his beloved mother. A function he has been taught to reverence as part of a religious practice, as the avenue whereby Immortality is gained, he will not abuse, to him it is Holy and Divine.

Laws are necessary for the control of evil; but no legal enactments, however drastic, will wipe out the degrading practice of prostitution, nor the social diseases, until the cause is eliminated. The treatment must be aimed at the roots of the cancerous growth, then there is hope of a cure.

The way to salvation is to instruct man in the truth; teach him all that concerns his creative function; both the reward of correct use and penalty of abuse. Prove to him that in right use is health, strength, success, and happiness; in abuse disease, weakness, misery, sorrow; the birth of idiots and perverts; finally damnation to himself and his progeny.

The Spiritual Significance of Sex

Part Two

Radicalism has been the curse of mankind in every age; from one extreme we swing to the other; either we respect neither law nor order, or we legislate every privilege out of existence; making of men, slaves.

Our understanding of all concerning sex has been irrational. For long centuries the sexual organism has been believed a shameful possession; thought of as unmentionable; the exercise of it indulged for pleasure and personal satisfaction; while the procreation of the specie has been mainly *accidental*. At last we are beginning to comprehend the potency and sacredness of sex; but with this enlightened understanding of the most important function native to the human being we are facing the spectacle of sex weaklings and human ice-bergs swinging to the chimerical and paranoiac extreme of inculcating not alone non-use of the function, but teaching the possibility of reaching physical immortality and the birth of children without the exercise of the function; first weakening the creative organism; finally degrading it; ending in the degeneration of the body and *destruction of the otherwise Immortal Soul.*

Although the degradation of sex in its many aspects is increasing alarmingly, very few of our citizens seem aware of it and as yet have no knowledge except that we are forced to contend with two destructive social diseases and the Red Light districts of our large cities, and, since the dispersion (by police power) of these segregated areas in cities, of separate houses, or small colonies, in the towns. Generally men and women are as yet unaware that the people are gradually becoming inoculated with a potential habit fruitful for the destruction of the race, through the inculcation of the phantasmal doctrine teaching that the separation of the sexes was a mistake, brought about through sin; that man shall find within himself the female, while woman should seek within herself the male; sex, as at present understood, becoming extinct, and children in the future born—the Lord knows how.

To the rational mind it seems highly improbable that such a fantastic idea could take root in the mentality of a people presumed to be well-balanced, but as an actual fact, we are being flooded with letters asking questions on the "how of this method," clearly indicating that many have become converted to the new "doctrine of death."

We are fully aware of the fact that a book written in the abstract and based on supposition, is seldom convincing, it therefore behooves us to deal with concrete instances. Before us we have a letter in which the writer, an intellectual woman widely known as a teacher, questions thus: "I do not believe any life can be happy and complete without Holy Matrimony, do you?" We readily answer; "*It cannot.*' But there is more to this letter, as follows: "Male and Female *in one.*" Here is the root of the trouble. This woman, coming in contact daily with many people, both men and women, and herself of a type capable readily to interest others, is continually inculcating the tenet that men and women once awakened, are complete within themselves and no longer require the opposite sex either as mates or companions; the solution to the enigma being obtainable, first, *through the non-exercise of the creative function; second, suppression of all desires, and aspiring to find the nature of the opposite sex within.*

As the rational mind can readily understand, the non-use and suppression, with such an idea in mind, has an action on the internal body similar to that resulting when we partly fill a barrel with fresh fruit juice, adding sugar and yeast, then tightly corking it. Just as soon as fermentation begins, a new force is created; this will produce an explosion; or, if the barrel is too strong, a gradual stagnation of the liquid takes place, ending in spoilation. In the human organism the non-use and suppression, which naturally includes retention, produces an irrita-

tion; this in turn an abnormal outlook on all life, finally inducing the hallucination of being one of those specially chosen by
God and anointed for the kingdom of eternal bliss.

The normal mind is incapable of conceiving the actual
mental attitude of one of these who labors under such a delusion;
we therefore quote extensively from a letter before us, bearing
date of December 4th, 1920.

"Masturbation and kindred practices, common in the
homes and out of them, all come out of the lusts of the flesh,
and have been stimulated just as much by legalized lust as by
unlegalized lust. By legalized lust I mean the coming together of a man and woman under the marriage law in the heat
of passion to gratify the flesh. This often results in the bringing forth of a child who is alike stimulated in his flesh with
ungodly passion, and eventually this apparently innocent child
(boy or girl) falls a victim of vice which has not been weeded
out through the incorporation of godly ideas. So long as parents
believe that legalized lust is sanctioned by not only the state,
but by God too, the case is hopeless."

Much of this is admittedly true and such instructions were
commendable to all; but directly after this sensible dissertation,
we are told:

"The truth to be taught is the Truth that Jesus Christ proclaimed—that when men are risen from the dead—that is, out of
the dream sleep of pleasure and pain in the senses, *that they
neither marry nor are given in marriage, neither do they die any
more (indulge in sex exchange or excitement of any nature) but
become as the angels in heaven—like unto the aspirational nature which is in the higher conscience of man.*"

Here is the key to the saving (?) philosophy taught by
this woman to large numbers of both sexes. It appeals to almost all of the cold-by-nature, neurotically emotional type of
people. It is admitted by physicians and investigators that we
are rapidly becoming a nation of neurasthenics; and to all of
these the denial of the creative nature, appeals; quickly winning

them over by the promise that they will "become as angels of heaven." We continue the quoting:

"But as the Master said, only those to whom it is given, can receive this Truth. Evidently it is not yet given to you to receive it. But as man purifies himself, willing to lose his life in order that he may find the Christ, God gives us the heaped up measure of Himself in idea, word, and act. Thus is God made manifest among men; and thus does the Word become flesh and dwell among us."

Drs. Freud and Ferenczi, world renowned Psycha-Analysists, have fully demonstrated that among the neurotic and neurasthenically emotional the appeal to martyrdom finds fertile soil, and the promise of "God made manifest" *in them* is inducive to almost any irrational action. Moreover, the statement directed at a student or correspondent that "evidently it is not yet given to *you* to receive it," would be an urge or incentive to "prove to the contrary." Thus one more novitiate is added to the fast increasing class of degenerates.

"If you knew the Philosophy of Life, or the history of the races, you would know that every root race experiences a change in the propagation of the Specie. We are going into the sixth root of the fifth root race, and are beginning to get ready for a higher kind of propagation."

Admittedly this is a crafty method of introducing the subject to those dissatisfied with present day religious life. Who of the many seeking the higher life is desirous of being known as a laggard? Ever aspiring to an existence more exalted than that universally lived, mankind is willing to offer some sacrifice whereby to be freed from the commonplace. Here is one who poses as a leader of those longing for "their souls' salvation," first offering the Theosophical chaff of the Root races, then slyly telling them (most knowingly) that with each root race the method of propagation changes; such a revolution being imminent; then proposing the plan, modestly admitting having a *foreknowledge* of all that God is about to consummate. Read further:

"According to the Creative Plan, the Sixth day is the bringing forth of the Ideal Man, the "image and likeness of God." *This Ideal Man is the man unified in the male and female nature* (italics by us), and so we see the doctrine of completeness in Christ, which when quickened in consciousness *forbids the expression of sex in the without.* The Son of Man is to be the outer manifestation of the One, not of the two."

In the "God forbids the expression of sex in the without, or Outer" we find the solution of the problem. What think all ye happily married, who, in your love one for the other, find peace, happiness and contentment, of such a philosophy of life? Is it not truly delightful to have one telling you that you are living without God, even though you are actually obedient to His commands "Love ye one another" and "Be ye fruitful and replenish the earth."

Many delude themselves with the belief that no one of sensible mind could possibly be deceived by such instructions. We wish our experience might justify such happy conclusions. Let us illustrate: Not long since there came to our office a buxom lassie of possibly twenty-two summers. This young lady gave us her story. Told us of not being physically well; of suffering from hot flushes, fainting spells, and otherwise not as she felt to be normal. Her appearance induced us to question her relative to conditions that ordinarily we would not have given a thought when verbally examining an unmarried woman to arrive at a diagnosis. After a time she admitted missing the menstrual flow for the past eight months, but stoutly maintained her innocence of any indiscreet action. Do what we would, question as we might, she would not admit ever having exercised the creative function; finally claiming that if she proved pregnant as we stated her to be, it must have been brought about by an *overshadowing of God.* Two weeks after her visit, she became the mother of a healthy and fully developed boy.

Did this girl honestly believe she could convince us that her pregnancy was the result of an overshadowing of God? If she did, what religious belief or philosophical inculcation hypnotized her into such a delusion? If this were the only instance of the kind we would be willing to think her irresponsible for her action; regrettable to admit, her case is merely one of many others.

Another experience is that of the consummation in happy marriage of a man twenty-six and a woman twenty-two years of age. Both parties well developed and certainly well-sexed. In the beginning all was as it should be with those harmoniously mated, but shortly after marriage they became acquainted with one who claimed ability to teach the Inner Spiritual development —the *awakening of the Soul*. Our friends, sensing the possibility of something higher in life than the mere physical, and seeking for wisdom, were readily induced to enroll with this propagandist.

The first requisite demanded of them was to forswear sexual indulgence. This was extremely difficult in their case, because, as previously stated, they were fitted with God's greatest blessing, *i. e.*, he with virile manhod, she with blessed womanhood. However, their desire for knowledge and the experience of an exalted life, prevailed, and they accepted the task of mastering the incentive of love. Though difficult, this was accomplished in a little more than one year; but they learned to their sorrow that as the desire for the marital embrace lessened, so their love for each other, likewise the longing to be in each others company, diminished.

After awakening to this disturbing fact, they too became aware that with the decrease in love for each other and the former yearning for the embrace, they had practically lost the aspiration for spirituality; finding themselves as two ships without rudders on a turbulent sea. In this predicament they consulted with us in the hope that we might be able to save them from what now appeared a horrible plight.* Since then we have had experience with many, many such cases, proving the delu-

---

* After finishing the chapter we received a letter from these people telling us they are stronger, healthier, and happier than ever before.

sion is becoming general. We will proceed with our quotations:

"God ordained marriage—the marriage of the Spirit and the soul to reproduce body. This marriage takes place in the consciousness and it cannot take place until sex has been met and overcome. The symbolic marriage in the without is a counterfeit expression of this inner union—the seeking of the male and female to blend as one in life and love so as to reproduce body. But they make a terrible fizzle of it as all life would indicate! All the rottenness of mortality comes out of this "most sacred relation" of men and women. However, when man separated his male and female nature, and later mixed with the "he and she animals" he set up conflict and strife and animal nature, and marriage as the world knows it has been his means of evoluting into more perfect form. But let no one deceive himself that it is the Creative Plan ordained by God. Jesus Christ culminated that Creative Plan, and I am doing so. I know what I am talking about, for I have traveled the Path that leadeth unto light."

Is it possible to display greater self-righteousness and egotism than this "female of the specie" here manifests? We frankly admit that in all our experience we have never had a more perfect illustration of the "holier than thou" attitude. Several of the statements are actually founded on truth, as for instance, man does reach his highest state of being when he develops within himself the feminine side of his nature. To speak clearly and understandingly, man should not merely be a business machine, cold-natured and devoted to mundane affairs; he ought also to allow that something within himself, termed the soul, which is capable of feeling love and compassion, and usually supposed peculiar to the feminine sex, to manifest. So with woman, instead of allowing the love and affection emotions to dominate her whole life, she should seek to attain tranquility by holding these in abeyance; thus permitting her to judge calmly and render decisions without allowing her sympathies to interfere. This is the *exact* meaning of the *Spiritual marriage*, and in no wise indicates that man shall be, or can be, sufficient unto himself, anymore than it is possible for woman to develop within herself the male who can impregnate her.

Marriage takes place in the consciousness, thus is born the enlightened Soul; but this does not prohibit marriage in the flesh between two who love each other; rather, it is an incentive to contract such a bond, thereby conferring upon a hungering world the blessings of a progeny born from the enlightened and exalted love union. It is likewise well for sex to be under control, but overcoming is *not* indicative of the destruction or deadening of the function; but *the controlling of it for wise and holy purposes; that is, for procreation, recreation, and regeneration;* all of these possible through the love union between man and woman.

It is altogether false that "all the rottenness of mortality" comes out of the "most sacred relationship." This is a lie, and a libel on God and His creation; and casts a stigma on all those who love each other and find health, strength, happiness and eventually Immortality, in their mutual love embraces. Admittedly, the sorrows of mortality spring from the sensual relationship between two people who seek each other only to the extent of indulging, but as frequently pointed out, that which can destroy life, can offer life; and the fact that an exercise is destructive to one is not the least indicative that it is harmful to another under different circumstances. Man no more separated himself from the female than did any of the other sexed creatures part one from the other. The creative law launched certain forces into motion, male and female were the result of the action. Moreover, it is not through any destructive practices, resultant from the vain hope of the female developing an impregnating male within herself, that the world is to be saved, but in the procreation of a new race by the embrace of men and women who truly love each other; and who have at heart the welfare of the race.

"The ancient order of the Essene Order* taught re-genera-

---

* The Therapeutae, members of the Essenian Order, were

tion through right and holy use of the sex forces (not the relation between men and women) as the means of bringing forth
the true son of Man. You distort the Truth of their teaching
either ignorantly or wilfully. I uncover your error not that
we may make much of the error, but that we may make much of
the Truth. "I come not to bring peace but the sword" wherever the sword needs to be laid at the root of the tree of de-
ception, trickery and falsehood. That falsehood has been over
man's eyes too long! My work is to uncover his eyes, so that
he may stand again before Jehovah God of his nature—
naked and unashamed, that is, clothed in truth."

Christianity has failed, and the sword has been the emblem of carnage, the destroyer of mankind; for no other reason
than such deceptive interpretations of Jesus' teachings. An
exposition of the Master's instructions such as that just quoted,
appeals to countless women who are weak and cold by nature;
constantly seeking for an avenue to escape their sacred duty toward God, husband, and family; likewise to men who are no
longer master of their creative function, consequently ready to
grasp at any straw offering an excuse for their weakness and
relieving them of a duty they find themselves unable to perform; being too imbecile to frankly admit their incapacity. Consider further:

"I teach in my course in Regeneration that Spirituality is
attained through the right and holy use of the sex force, that is,
its transmutation in the individual to beget the life and love of
God which will clothe man in living soul, and eventually in living body. "The two that were joined in God must become one
in flesh." The two that are joined by the laws of the world
are not one flesh, but are separated, each seeking to devour each
other with ungodly desire and longings. Their desire is for

---

allowed to marry. The writer labors under a delusion as to what
this ancient Order really did teach. Moreover, we are privileged to
here state that she does not possess the knowledge of what the
Essenes did, or did not, inculcate in their ritual and philosophy.
See "Philosophy of Fire," Philosophical Publishing Co., Quakertown, Pa.

God, their longing for the perfect union of the male and female within consciousness, but they cannot have it so long as they function in sex. Thank God, that the laws of Divine Love forbids man's entrance into the Garden of Eden and its heavenly bliss until he has passed the "flaming-sword" at the entrance which turns in every direction to keep intact the tree of life until he is pure enough to receive it."

The pity of it! Of the many now sincerely seeking to *know* the Father and to gain *Conscious union* between their Soul and God, and the linking of the male and female nature (not person) in their own being, an unknown number will be led astray by listening to such delusitory instructions; not awakening to their danger until, through suppression, they have burned up the springs of *living water* within themselves and become either imbeciles or perverts. Man, nor woman, is unable to reach Immortality by such a destructive process; nor can the Garden of Eden be so entered. *Love only is the key to that garden,* and such love must be manifested by true affection and all this implies, between man and woman, *and of both for God.*

Consider the new and painless method for the propagation of the specie, as taught by this new Avatar who so knowingly tells us God's plans:

"The manner of bringing forth children in the Sixth Root race is clearly revealed to me. I explained it to my class last night. We are studying the Third Chapter of Genesis and clarifying consciousness on many points. You should have heard the class, then you would not be anxious about how the Ideal Man is to be born, nor how he is to be housed. One thing I can assure you, the Ideal Man, like Jesus, will be born above the "ways of men" (men, being the state of consciousness formed through the action of adulterated thought). Mary had to rebel against the modern methods of maternity before she could sing her Mary (merry) song, "My soul doth magnify the Lord, and my Spirit hath rejoiced in Christ, my Saviour." Christ is the saviour in this day as it was in the days of Mary—

and Jesus Christ is to be the body that is to manifest—the body of Christ ideas."

One might smile and jeer at such an exposition of the most sacred relationship that can exist between man and woman, with its possibility of linking them directly with humanity and God, were it not for the knowledge that the number deluded by such doctrines is increasing daily, despite the fact that none of these disciples of the blind and misleading leaders has ever been enabled to materialize "one of the flesh out of the Spirit," and that not a single one has manifested health, strength, vitality, happiness, or real success.

The Youth and Sex

By commencing to instruct the boy yet in his youth, that the creative function is basically religious, encircles in love and truth just as is prayer and all other worship of God, and continuing the inculcation until he reaches the age of responsibility; by further instilling into his mind that the greatest curse under which mankind has bowed for ages and suffered, is man's inhumaneness in demanding and accepting favors from a woman he does not love; that the only motive permitting sexual congress is love and a desire for the Immortalization of the Soul of both parties; there need be no fear that he will prostitute his creative potencies; little danger of his contracting any of the loathsome and degrading diseases now so prevalent.

Babylonianism

The Straighest Road to Damnation

Very few writers of the past have had the courage to speak plainly on the depraved practices (sins) which were basically the cause of the fall and destruction of Babylon. This entire subject, disgusting as it unquestionably is, is no longer avoidable owing to the various writings and publication of several books by a physician of standing, whose instructions, if to any great extent practiced, will quickly result in the degeneration of the entire race, destroying man, *body and soul.*

It is essential for us to quote *verbatim* from one of these books, so that we may comment on his "inculcations of fraud," though we will attempt to eliminate abhorrent words and phrases by substituting words less repulsive; these will appear in *italics.*

"The hand of the opposite sex will produce effects on the genitals of the other which will not be produced in any other way. Thus, a man may hold his *glans* in his own hand for a given length of time, longer or shorter, and no results will be effected, no secretion of the prostatic fluid be made, at all. But let the wife take *this* in her hand for the same length of time, and the flow of the prostatic fluid will at once take place. This is true whether the *glans* be erect or detumescent (*relaxed*). If the wife will hold her husband's limp *glans* in her hand for but a few minutes, even though the organ remains limp, the flow of the prostatic fluid will take place. The same is true with regard to the husband's putting his hand on his wife's vulva. Should she hold her hand there, no pre-coital fluid would be secreted.

With her husband's hand there, the flow would at once begin.

"This is a remarkable physical and psychological phenomenon, and it is one especially worthy of note. It is this fact that makes mutual masturbation far superior to auto-erotism. A husband can thus satisfy a wife with his fingers, or a wife her husband with her hand, far better than either could bring herself or himself to the climax alone. This point is of great import, in considering many of the sex acts of husband and wife.

"As a rule, let the husband and wife do whatever their desire prompts or suggests, and just as they feel they would like to. Only this, let all be in moderation. Carry nothing to excess!"

Neither Sodom, Gomorrha, or Babylon ever formulated a practice more damnable and destructive than this. Because of its apparent innocence it quickly seduces its victims and degrades them beyond redemption before they are aware that the mutual fraud is destroying body and soul. Like solitary vice, the practice readily becomes a habit, and once established is far more difficult to overcome than ordinary harlotry.

The great sin is not so much in the mutual play itself, as in the *soul searing* deed of "casting the seed upon the ground." We have already treated at length on the results of this act, illustrating it by the experience of the Israelites when on their way to the Promised Land; and it would seem that we, in what should be a sane and enlightened age, are to *react the carnage of lust of which the ancient people were guilty, destroying their body and soul, the greater number of them.*

Time and again we have emphasized the *absolutely irrevocable law* that the marriage rite may be indulged only for three purposes: Procreation, Recreation, and Regeneration. It is Divinely forbidden for man and woman to seek gratification merely for self-satisfaction or pleasure. To attempt this is certain to bring a heavy penalty; though some good is obtained in the normal embrace, as for instance, the exchange of the magnetic-electric forces between husband and wife. This may be made an excuse, but the *demonic* practice of *exterior sex demonstration* which this extensively read author advocates, cannot be justified by either law or reason; is admittedly purely for carnal (therefore destructive) sense gratification; damned by God and *every* Creative Law; quickly dulling the moral sense so that men and women guilty of it fall to below the animal plane; becoming brutish, shameless creatures, lacking understanding of the meaning of Love and all related to it.

God, during primary creation, acted wisely when he so constituted man that an abuse of the sexual function would likewise be detrimental to the Mind and Soul; that a wasting of the seminal fluid, whether by conjugal fraud or this advocated mutual masturbation, would also be a loss of brain power; ultimately resulting in idiocy and the *destruction of the soul, making life after death utterly impossible.* In truth, making it far easier for the elephant to pass through the eye of a needle, *than for two creatures, possessing human forms, who mutually abuse—and destroy—each other, to enter the kingdom.*

If the church ever had a duty to perform then it is this—to hurl, with all its might, a *pronunciamento* against this practice.

Admittedly the fondling of the creative organism of the husband by the wife does quickly induce the prostatic fluids to flow, as likewise will the husband's touch release the pre-coital flow in the woman, but for this very reason this is to be avoided at all times, except as a preliminary to the marriage rite; even at these periods great care should be exercised not to continue the fondling for too long a time, lest it weakens the strength of one or the other of the participants; is permissible only until both parties are ready for the embrace.

We emphatically contradict that release of the prostatic fluid in the male, and the pre-coital lochia in the female, under such excitation is a remarkable physical phenomena. Psychological it undoubtedly is, but not in the least mysterious; because the youth when sexually anhungered, can, by the mere play of his imagination, see himself in relation with some fancied companion, and thereby induce a prostatic flow. Many girls and women have confessed to us being able to do likewise. It is therefore nothing more or less than the arousing of the physical creative desires by awakening the imaginative faculty to a degree necessary to produce the flow and consequent relaxation; *it is self fraud.* To continue our quotation:

"Let it be said further, that auto-erotism, self-spending, may be practiced by both men and women, to their healthful benefit, when sexual excitement cannot be secured in any other way. It is only when carried to excess that such action is in any way harmful. The only danger is, that, the individual being alone and having all the means for self-gratification in his or her own hands, so to speak, it is quite possible to indulge in the action too freely, which, of course, leads to bad results. *But the act itself is not bad.* On the contrary, when kept within bounds, it is healthful and wholesome."

Clearly our learned author is illogical. Previously he admitted that *mutual* masturbation is more desirable and pleasurable than solitary vice; now he tells us that the individual, having all the means at hand, may over-indulge. If it is true that mutually *committing the crime*— we say "committing the crime" advisably— gives greater pleasure than the solitary act, and if self-spending—more correctly termed "self-pollution"—is vice-forming, then how much more so is the intensely pleasure-giving double criminal act?

Auto-erotism, so termed because even the habitues to it are ashamed to apply its rightly designated appellation—masturbation or self-pollution,—is a crime against the self and God. Every "fall" is resultant of the "casting upon the ground" of millions of "seed" which would either help in the creation of a new being if properly consigned, or in the recreation of the self-being if transmuted; that being undesirable for the moment, then the rejuvenation of the two beings taking part in the exchange in the lawful manner.

Self-pollution is a crime because it sets at variance *every creative law,* and all guilty of the pernicious practice are thereafter ashamed to look themselves squarely in the eyes by the aid of a mirror; as well as being unable to face their fellow creatures.

It is only when continued for a length of time sufficient to break down the moral stamina, indicating likewise a loss of brain and soul force, that the practitioner of solitary vice or mutual masturbation, becomes *blase* enough to face his own emaciated self and the world at large, without pangs of conscience.

The practice is demoralizing even if indulged but once, because through that one act a certain amount of vital force is cast aside without the possibility of recovery. It is giving something and receiving nothing, therefore robbery of the self, so destructive. The more frequently the function is exercised in this morally prohibited manner, the nearer man, or woman, draws to the brink of moral degradation and physical imbecility. The act in itself is evil; it is debasing; unfitting *every* man who is guilty, to meet face to face any pure woman; not mentioning the possibility of meeting the Giver of Life. Listen further:

"There are many unmarried women, maiden ladies, and especially widows, who would greatly improve their health if they practiced some form of auto-erotism, occasionally."

We personally wish to appear on record as voicing the sentiment, that if the sexual desire of any woman, whether maiden lady or widow, become so insistent that relief is actually necessary, then it would be *far* better for them, body and soul, and the world at large, to follow the old religious practice of the maidens of India—veil their faces and sit before the temple, accepting the offer of the first man that passes. Thus would the relief sought be obtained; seed would not be cast upon the ground; and such would receive in exchange an amount of vital magnetic force equal to that expended by their creative organism. We do not advocate such method of seeking freedom from the thraldom of passion, but we do maintain that if relief must be obtained, this would be a thousand-fold preferable to the seed-wasting, disease-inducing, lust-engendering, practice of self-pollution advocated by Dr. L. Consider further:

"As a matter of fact, all boys masturbate, and many girls also. Some authors claim that more than half of the women engage in some form of auto-erotism, at some time in their lives, and the estimate is probably too low rather than too high. But unless they carry the act to excess, they are guilty of no wrong. Not infrequently, they may make the act a means of great good to themselves. The sex organs are alive! They constantly secrete fluids that need to be excreted, as all other organs of the body do. They ought to be relieved, as their nature requires they should be."

It is utterly false that all boys are guilty of self-pollution. Admittedly the majority are, ignorantly so, but this does not permit any man the license to damn every one of the male sex. Likewise it is true that many girls are victims of the habit, and with what results? We have known of women who indulged in the destructive practice before they were married, and when wedded preferred it to the natural creative embrace; allowing their husbands to caress and fondle them until their desires were fully aroused, then turning the cold shoulder to them,—defrauding both themselves and their husbands by a recurrence to the old degrading habit. Can any one imagine anything more abominable than this? Yet this is what perverters of human virtues inculcate.

Admittedly the sexual organism is an active entity; constantly secreting fluids which are life-giving; it being essential to health and well-being to keep these vital forces in circulation; but this offers no permission to destroy them; it is merely an indication they should be naturally utilized; the method being either through a reabsorption into the circulation and a transmutation into mental and soul forces; or an exchange between the male and female. God created the two, male and female created He them; He comprehended that neither one nor the other could possibly be sufficient unto himself, consequently He mated them, that one might seek the other. Auto-erotism is a crime greater than murder or patricide, because the practice destroys the *self*, and redemption then becomes impossible. We quote again:

"Sometimes, during the five days of menstruation, during which time the union of the organs is deemed not best, the wife can thus help her lover with her hand, to the delight and benefit."

We would inquire, what of the woman during this period? If he suffers, how much greater must be the longing on her part as she fondles him, but yet is denied all relief?

Undeniably there are men so strong in their virility that they keenly feel the deprivation of exercise during these few days, but if they are mentally developed in proportion to their manhood, and not merely male animals, they gladly suffer temporarily because the possibilities for love become so much greater and intensified during the short period of waiting. As a matter of fact, we find that the true man looks forward to these temporary rests in the knowledge that there will be greater satisfaction to both after the interval of waiting.

If any man is so weak mentally and morally to be unable to control the desires during the period of her cleansing, that he must be guilty of self-pollution, then it would be far better for him to avoid all association with the woman by sleeping in a separate bed, or that failing, do just as the animals in the field—disgustingly cohabiting during the lunar season, and be stamped with the marks of Cain. This would actually not be as grievous a sin as the one-sided auto-erotism.

Greece, once the most enlightened and cultured nation on the face of the earth, fell into decadence through the Cult of Sappho. Sappho, the poetess, like our Dr. L., taught the practice of mutual masturbation and ora-erotism, and gradually these debaucheries became so universal that parents who foresaw the end of the race because of it, paid their maids to become the mothers of their sons' children; all to no avail, the prostitution of the creative power had become so extended the race was doomed.

Babylonia, one of the centers of the richest, proudest, and most cultured races then on earth met its doom through similar practices. The degradation finally reaching the stage where the lips served the purpose of the *labiae* Major and Minor. Noted Divines preach on the destruction of Babylon and of the wickedness of its people, but are extremely reticent in mentioning what these sins really were, either ignorant or unmindful of the fact that cults in America are becoming numerous who inculcate and practice these identical sins.

Sodom and Gomorrha were destroyed by the Lord; "burned up" by the sexual excesses of its inhabitants. Men became the lovers of their sex; women preferred women, fondling with the hands as now openly advocated by some physicians in America soon became too refined for them; lips were resorted to; and pro-creation ceased, finally, Lot alone was the father of a family.

Greece, Egypt, Sodom and Gomorrha, Babylonia and Rome all trace their destruction to the debasing practices having their inception in the inculcation and practice of demonical rites such as advocated by our Dr. L. and others seeking the maximum of pleasure with the minimum of responsibility. Multitudes, especially men and women who desire the pleasures of sexual excitement, but shun the responsibilities of parentage, are easily led to believe there is no harm in such practices. Gradually and insidiously it masters them; to one *mode of procedure* out of the natural, is added another until at last none satisfy and they are first the victims, then the perpetuators and inculcators of the most hideous vices malicious minds can conceive.

Is America, the proud nation over which the Eagle takes its flight, to have a list of thousands of ultra-cultured people guilty of all the sex abuses cataloguable, as had England during the world war?

Is America to begin the downward path toward doom, similar to that of Greece, Rome and other past great nations? From the present trend, judging by the contents of books and magazines dealing with sex life now sold, we are to meet a similar fate.

Conjugal Fraud

Destroying Marital Happiness

Apparently Dr. L., the author so generously quoted in the former chapter, is not merely the high priest of the *cultus auto-erotics;* of singly and mutual pollution; but equally so of the universal wrecker of marital happiness, termed conjugal fraud.

Under the caption "Coitus Reservatus," meaning the commencement of the marriage rite in harmony with nature's dictates, proceeding almost to the climax, then discontinuing for the time being, he tells us:

"It should be the constant aim and endeavor of both parties to continually lift all sex affairs above the plane of animality, mere physical gratification, into the realm of mental and spiritual delight." This has our hearty approval; being in entire harmony with all that we teach in this and former books. Unhappily, he continues:

"To this end, let it be said at once that such a condition can be reached, in the greatest degree, by the practice of what is known, in scientific terms, as *"coitus reservatus,"* which, translated, means going only *part* of the way in the act, and not carrying it to its climax, the organism (*orgasm*). Described in terms with which the reader is now familiar, it means, carrying the act only through the first and second stages, the "courting stage," in common parlance, teasing, "and the union of the organs, and stopping there!"

"Going a bit into details, this act of "reservatus" really unites the first two parts of the act into a common whole, making it simply one continuous piece of "courting," merely that, and nothing more.

"To engage in this form of coitus, not nearly the effort should be made to arouse the sexual passions of either of the parties, as has already been described as fitting for complete coitus. The organism (*orgasm*) is not the desideratum in this case, but it is just a delightful expression of mutual love. It is a sort of prolonged and all-embracing kiss, in which the sex organs are included as well as the lips. They kiss each other as the lips kiss each other. It is "courting," par excellence, without the hampering of clothes or conventionality of any kind."

Here we have a perfect example of the modern method of procedure in conjugal fraud, one of the most damnable practices now cursing the marriage relationship, totally contrary to every law of nature in both the human and subhuman realm and not one word can be said in its favor.

As the practice of mutual masturbation previously considered, destroys the parties participating by draining them gradually of their virile force without replacing it through exchange, so does this defrauding burn up the body and soul, because of the *centering of the creative forces for the purpose of both relief and exchange*, only to be denied expression at the last moment.

Dr. L. does not actually believe his own instructions. In speaking of the male weakling, who has not sufficient manly strength to satisfy the longings of his mate, he writes:

"After a man has passed the orgasm, it is, in most cases, impossible for him to continue the act, right then and there, and bring the woman to the climax, if she has not yet arrived, from the fact that, with the expulsion of the semen, usually detumerescence of the *glans* at once takes place, and the organ is incapable of exciting the woman when in this condition. And so, if the husband *"is ahead" first*, there is no possibility of the wife's reaching the climax at that embrace. *This leaves her unsatisfied, all her sex organs congested, and the whole situation is unsatisfactory, in the extreme.*"

We fully concur in these statements, they express exact facts, and we have italicized them to call the reader's special attention to the truths voiced; thus clearly indicating how inconsistent is the average writer on these subjects, and how illogical his conclusions.

In instances of indulgence in the sexual embrace, where the strength of the husband is insufficient for the satisfaction of his wife, forcing him to discontinue the marriage rite before she reaches the climax, he at least bathes her creative organism with the seminal fluid; doing much toward reducing the inflammation and irritation resulting from unsatisfied desire; but in conjugal fraud, termed "reservatus," not even this occurs; the congested, inflamed organism being forced to attempt gradually "throwing back" into circulation the blood and fluids which were held ready for expulsion and exchange at the crisis; and has to contend with the after-irritation without the soothing serums to relieve the intensity of it. If, as the author admits, *and we maintain as true*, the unsatisfied desire of the wife and consequent congestion has serious results on her health, how much greater, think you, is the continuous congesting and resultant irritation following the repeated conjugal fraud (reservatus) suggested; and not followed by the cooling and healing effects of being bathed by the seminal fluid?

We have personally treated, and listened to the confessions of thousands of women suffering from the effects of love-hunger as the result of weakness in the husbands. These wives were to be pitied, but could be helped by careful instructions; in most instances they accepted the situation, being mindful of the "for better or for worse" of the marriage ceremony; respecting their husbands, believing them blameless. At the same time, we have come in close relationship with an almost equal number of women whose husbands continually defraud them by "coitus reservatus;" most of these poor wives are beyond hope; having lost faith in nature, man and God; and "burned out" like hollow trees ravished by forest fires; the inner spirit crushed and shrunken; the Soul seared and distorted; sex itself become the serpent creeping in the dust on its belly; like it, cursed by God. Even these can be saved if they are willing to obey, but most of them are no longer possessed of sufficient stamina to make the required effort toward self-redemption.

In the quotation to follow, the author foolishly believes he is offering credulous mankind the key to the Paradise of Love, when, as a fact, he is instructing it in the most direct route to *Prostatic ailments,* the most dreadful ravages from which man can suffer; frequently termed the "hell-fire" of middle to old age.

"This method is of special service during the 'unfree time.' If rightly used, it will not tend to increase the desire for 'spending,' but it will, on the contrary, allay and satisfy the sexual desires, most perfectly. If, while learning how, sometimes the inexperienced should 'get run away with,' and feel that it is better to go on and have the climax, all right. But, as time goes on, the practice of carrying the act only to the end of the second part, will grow, and in due time will be well established. Those who have mastered this wholesome and loving art will sometimes meet in this way a score of times during a month or so, without once coming to the climax."

It is illogical to claim that any organs as sensitive as those of the creative system can be brought to the highest state of expectancy, thoroughly infused, and then allowed to remain in that condition by refusal to give them relief, will allay and satisfy the desire. Any one who has ever attempted this is aware that there is an intense feeling of uneasiness in the parts, inducing a physical and mental unrest which nothing but a normal and fully completed embrace can relieve. Admittedly, if this practice is continued for any length of time and in the manner suggested, it will become established and apparently satisfactory, but this is due to the weakening of the internal forces and the gradual loss of sensitiveness of the entire creative organism; a process of "burning up," as results from the over-heating, without properly tempering, of any sensitive material substance.

Any one posing as the inculcator of an art, or a method, should be at least consistent, but the author of this special system for the destruction of body and soul contradicts himself frequently, as note the following.

"* * * , if it should sometimes happen that the husband should arrive at the climax before the wife does, and he could not bring her to an organism (*orgasm*) by excitation with the spent *glans,* it would be perfectly right for him to substitute his finger, and satisfy her in that way. Of course, this would not be as satisfying to her as it would have been could she have met him simultaneously, but it is far better than for her not to be entirely satisfied. *Many a woman suffers all night long with unsatisfied desire, her organs congested and tumescent, because she has been left unsatisfied by a husband who has spent before she was ready, and then left her!* Such cases might be entirely relieved, if the parties knew the truth, and were not too ignorant, or prejudiced, or ashamed, to do what should be done to make the best of a situation."

In one paragraph we are informed in detail how the embrace may be commenced, the act carried to almost the climax, and then discontinued, without increasing the desire for indulgence; on the contrary, allaying and satisfying the sexual appetite; in due time becoming established and a normal act; while in the next he tells us of the suffering resulting to a woman when her desires remain unsatisfied, because of not being brought to the climax. These contradictions are met throughout the book, but do not render its several inculcations any the less dangerous because the ordinary reader, seeking a method offering the gratification of lust without obliging him to reap undesirable results, will not be apt to note these contradictions.

We heartily concur in the statement relative to the desirability of relieving the suffering of the woman resultant on her not being brought to the climax, but have never known of the necessity for semi-erotic practices on the part of the husband; even a weakling can be instructed in natural methods, making it possible for him to perform his manly conjugal duties with entire satisfaction.

Dr. L's advice to the single is on a par with that offered the married, as note the following:

"If a bride and bridegroom knew enough to introduce each other to the delights of an organism (*orgasm*) by "spending" each other by external excitation of the organs with their hands a few times before they united the organs at all, it would be to their lasting well-being. This is especially true for the bride. If her lover would take her in his arms, even with all her clothes on, as she sat on his lap, in their bridal chamber, alone, and stroked her vulva till she "spent," the chances are many to one that he would have introduced her to such joy that she would never forget it, all her life."

It is inconceivable that any one living in the present century and possessing the education required to pass the strict examinations of a Medical College, could possibly be guilty of inditing such unhuman, minus-animal, super-brute instructions as these. Let the father who, adoring his daughter and believing her innocence personified, feeling assured of having entrusted her into the care of a man who will protect her from all that is evil and degrading; and who desiring to embrace her, will first caress and fondle her, thus preparing her before proceeding in God's most holy manner to exercise the creative function, picture in his mind this girl with her purity of mind, unsullied body, and chastity of sex, sitting on the lap of this man, actually such only in designation, who proceeds to masturbate—an ugly word, but here justified—her, and what will he do?

If there is any moral stamina, and desire for the protection of the pure and innocent, in his heart, the degenerate whom law recognizes as his son-in-law, will not live to degrade another innocent girl; he would contend it beyond contradiction that any man who will commit this crime— crime it is—on an ignorant and unsuspecting girl, will not long be satisfied after he has so defiled her, but quickly seek another victim that his foul lust be appeased. We seriously question whether even Dr. L. would instruct his daughter, if he has any, to permit such pollution of her person.

Whether such a soul-shattering practice brings a "joy to her that she would never forget, all her life" depends entirely upon the morality and *finesse* of her character. If she is one begotten in a family where vulgarity is the rule of character, she may accept it as a natural incident, one to be expected; but if a girl-woman such as we have in mind, as hoping our daughter to be, she would slap the brute across the face, damn his soul to perdition, and seek relief in a Court of Justice.

The one thing in life that the young man looks forward to and a consummation he *never forgets,* is the entering of the *great unknown*—the first complete marriage embrace he enjoys with his bride. Were such a practice indulged, the Rite following would be a farce, a parody on the Divine creative act. Consider further:

"Indeed, if a bride to be, who was so innocent or ignorant of her sex possibilities that she had never experienced an organism (*orgasm*)—had never "spent"—could be "put wise" before her bridal night, if she could be instructed enough to lead her to engage in some form of auto-erotism, bringing herself to an *orgasm* with her own hand, just for the sake of the experience it would give her, and so that she would have some clear idea of what she really wanted, before she went into the arms of her lover —if she could do this, in the right mental attitude, it would be greatly to her well-being, a worthy and valuable addition to her stock of knowledge of herself and of the powers that are latent within her. Her alleged loss of innocence by such an act would be nothing compared with the wisdom she would gain by the experience."

All established churches have inculcated the doctrine that the Serpent of Satan once in the Garden of Eden, no longer existed; however, it is our firm opinion that if that particular serpent died, then Satan (personified evil) has been enabled to create one far superior to the original tempter; such instructions for the defilement of the innocent, emanating from it.

Apparently it is not sufficiently destructive to the race that many of our finest girls fall victims to the habit of self-abuse, totally ignorant of the penalty to be paid later; we must now witness the spectacle of writers, accepted as authorities, teaching self-pollution to our maidens, deluding them into the belief the experience is necessary and a correct method of obtaining wisdom.

Unquestionably such practices add both experience and

wisdom to the sum total of the girl's possessions; but they like-wise affix the constant reminder of degradation and self-pollu-tion; a feeling of uncleanliness, and an incapacity to look into the eyes of the innocent youth without the ever-present thought of unworthiness. Girls who fall victims to the habit through the machinations of others equally guilty, can readily be for-given; theirs is not a conscious guilt; but for the girl who delib-erately degrades her most sacred treasure, there can be no excuse.

We venture to say that if actual knowledge and experience is essential to the welfare of his daughter, the average father who is also a man in the true sense of the term, would far prefer to see his daughter in the arms of a clean man, even though he is not her husband, and the embrace righteously con-summated, thus permitting them the continued freedom of being able to face their fellow-being and God without shame, than to know her guilty of this shameful practice. The latter is damned by God, causing the actor to hide the face with shame, while the former is Nature's method for the relief of the person, the gain-ing of knowledge, and the exchange of Love, though possibly not ethically sanctioned. We read further:

"The fact is, this whole matter of sexual excitation by means of the hand, or in any other way than the union of the organs, has received a black eye at the hands of would-be purists, which it in no way deserves. As already noted, the word masturbation has been fastened to such acts, and then, any and every form of it has been condemned far beyond what the facts warrant, till the minds of the rank and file are wholly misled in the premises! When one looks at the situation from the point of view which insists that all the sex functions should be under the control of the will, then light is thrown upon the entire subject. Seen in this way, any form of sex stimulation, or auto-erotism (auto-erotism means *self-excitation*) which is not carried to excess, is right and wholesome."

In answering this, we reiterate former statements:

First, any attempt to relieve the creative organism from the vital, or seminal fluids, other than by the union of the male and female organisms, having in mind at the same time some elevating purpose, is self-abuse, self-pollution, and damned by God and all chaste minds.

Second, I am not a purist, nor a would-be purist, I consider all God created as pure and holy, and its right use sanctioned by Him; but self-satisfaction in any form which necessitates the "casting of the seed upon the ground" I maintain is defrauding the self and God; therefore destructive to body and soul alike; making of man eventually less than the lowest creature of the field.

Third, let us thank God with our whole hearts that the rank and file are not yet inoculated with the practice of the "beasts" of Sodom, Gomorrha and Babylon. They are *not* misled, they merely have been fortunate in remaining uninitiated in the "rites that damn the soul." Let us hope they never will be.

Fourth, there is a vast difference between sex stimulation and self-gratification, by this writer termed "auto-erotism." "Sex stimulation" is properly applied to the method of arousing the self or one's partner to an intense desire for the embrace. This is natural, normal and desirable, and may be properly termed the display of affection and endearments. Auto-erotism is plain, every-day masturbation; a practice shunned by all clean-minded men and women.

Fifth, self-gratification is *never* wholesome; is *always* degrading and destructive. Should be avoided as the devil is said to flee holy water.

Sixth, the creative law permits the excitation of the sexual organism only for the purpose of arousing the desire of the dormant party who is to become one of the participants in the divine drama, and when this is accomplished, the union must take place; nor dare it be discontinued until both parties are satisfied. To do otherwise is to commit conjugal fraud and will certainly arouse the disgust of the one defrauded. The seminal fluid has for its purpose, aside from procreation, the "charging" of the entire person of the female; just as a current from a dynamo charges the cells of a battery; thus inducing quiescence to her entire nervous system; while the magnetic forces carried by her lochia has an equally great influence on his mentality.

Seventh, life and death are hidden in the creative embrace. It is the original "Tree of Life" in the Garden of Eden. Self-satisfaction, mutual erotism, and conjugal fraud are death-dealing to body and soul. Mutual desire, mutual satisfaction, based on love between the two taking part in the marital rite. gives health, strength and greater love for each other; finally salvation of the soul. Take your choice, you are a free moral agent.

The Menace

"Captains of industry cry that we must speed up production in our factories, but there is just as urgent a need that we hasten the production of food on our farms.

"Conditions in our agricultural sections were in a sad way before we entered the war, but soon after we joined the conflict they became very serious. Lured by the high wages being paid by the big war industries, thousands of farmers and their sons deserted their farm lands and flocked to the cities. Of all the farm lads who went into the army and navy it is reported that not more than two per cent. of them have returned to the farms again.

"Today we have *seventy* per cent. of our people crowded into the cities and but thirty per cent. in the country. That means that every three persons living on a farm must produce enough to eat not only for themselves, but for seven other city people, to say nothing of the millions of tons of food for export.

"It is estimated that more than 1,000,000 persons have moved away from the farms in the last three years. In Michigan there are 30,000 vacant farmhouses; in New York State, 24,000 more empty farm homesteads. Our own Pennsylvania tables usually are abundantly supplied from the farms and gardens of Pennsylvania, New Jersey and Delaware. Yet Pennsylvania today reports a 37 per cent. shortage of farm labor, New Jersey, 23 per cent. and Delaware, 40 per cent. In New Jersey they are paying high school boys four dollars per day on the fruit and vegetable farms." *Bernhard Orstralink, Director National Farm School, "The Philadelphia Inquirer," October* 3, 1920.

COUNTRY ROBBERY AND CITY STARVATION

"A farmer in southern Michigan sold first grade apples last October for 60 cents a bushel, after paying $5.00 a day to apple pickers. In nearby cities similar apples were selling for $3.00 a bushel.

"A farmer in southwestern New York shipped 29 barrels of pears to market. He received from the commission house to which the pears were shipped, a check for $26.00 in full payment for the pears. Similar pears were being retailed in New York and Philadelphia for several dollars a bushel.

"Near Duluth, Minnesota, a farmer raised a fine field of cabbage in 1919. He sold it to a commission house in Chicago. *The cabbage rotted in the field.*

"While Hogs are selling at the Chicago stockyards as low as $10.00 a hundred, pork tenderloin is being retailed in Des Moines for *$1.00 a pound.*

"These cases are cited to show present marketing conditions. *The producer is not receiving enough in many cases to cover cost of production, but the consumer in the city is paying extortionate prices.* It matters not where you live, your pocketbook is being robbed while such conditions exist and the entire prosperity of the country is gravely affected." *"The People's Popular Monthly." January, 1921.*

Italics are ours to emphasize the reasons for many present almost unbearable conditions. Readers of the book may reasonably question how these several items can have any bearing on the question of sex. They are introductory to the chapter on "Birth Control" and prove some of the assertions.

Birth Control

Preface: We emphatically affirm that Birth Control as at present advocated by the many more or less distinguished *foreign* representatives of the Neo-Malthusian cult, and the American high-priestess of this foreign spawn, is doubly dangerous to the white race.

First: The methods taught are often degrading to the mentality of the actors; ruinous to the physical being; and if pregnancy results despite the means followed, as it *often* does, is productive of weaklings, criminals, and perverts; frequently insane. It shatters the health, especially of the woman, because the contraceptions are ofttimes such that destroy the *vital forces* in the seminal fluids and she is defrauded; while in many other instances the practice pursued for the prevention of conception is worse even than mutual masturbation, breeding disgust in the ones indulging.

Second: The white race today composes less than one third of the total inhabitants of the known world and were it not for the aggressiveness and greater incentive of the white race, it would now be doomed. As it is, even with its present birth rate, the combined colored races are increasing two to one; with the awakening of these races to western methods of manufacture and warfare, it is merely a question of a few years when their supremacy will have become established.

Third: The white race, as demonstrated in Holland, France, and other countries where race suicide cults have taken firm root, quickly accepts the practice, while the colored races never will; being fully conversant that with numbers at their command, and the knowledge they are rapidly acquiring of the methods of life and warfare of the white race, they can gradually emigrate to the countries of the white race and subjugate it. This is not a fanatic's dream; all the statistics bear out our assertion of the rapid increase of the colored races; likewise of their rapidly increasing proficiency in the sciences, arts, and all belonging to the practice of warfare; while it is long since admitted they are superior in craftiness and secrecy, and in the propagation of the specie are more than the white man's equal.

Our Platform: Race Control should be permissible, even advocated, when:

First: The male is afflicted with a communicable disease such as Syphilis, or some other form of degeneracy or mental weakness; when the female is not physically strong, or suffering from cancer, tuberculosis, some form of blood disease, or is mentally irresponsible.

Second: The family is sufficiently large, requiring all the efforts of the father to support it properly and giving it the educational and social advantages such as should undeniably be the portion of every child born.

Any other excuse is illogical and illegitimate, and savors of a desire to enjoy the pleasures of the marital relationship without possessing the strength of character to accept the responsibilities resultant of the contract.

The advocates of Birth Control offer a thousand and one other excuses for their activities as clearly indicated and readily proven by their own writings, and in this Chapter we propose to quote extensively from the writings of Mrs. Sanger and her associates; offering our comments; allowing the reader to accept or refuse the conclusions.

It is perfectly legitimate for the physician to prescribe a poisonous drug when, in his opinion, it is indicated; but it is criminal for him to do so when the gravity of the case does not actually demand it, doing so merely to relieve the patient from some responsibility. Birth Control is just as criminal when there is no valid reason for it.

In an Editorial by Margaret Sanger appearing in "The Birth Control Review," January 1920, we read:

"The world faces its greatest crisis. It approaches the

greatest disaster of all times. And even before the arrival of that disaster, children are being worked to death in American factories; they are being starved in countless numbers in Europe.

"Hunger has not yet gripped the United States as a nation, but we are no longer a nation to ourselves. We must feed Europe, and Europe's hunger is bound to reflect itself upon us. Already we have felt the first nip of deprivation in high prices and the scarcity of a number of food products. And as Europe's condition gets worse, so too will ours grow worse."

In these several paragraphs there is not a single logical reason for the need of Birth Control; rather the contrary. It is true that in our own America children are being worked to death, enslaved body and soul; but this is *not* due to an insufficiency of food, but *because of the physical, mental and moral depravity of many Americans.* Generally, nay, in most instances, these children are working in factories wherein are being manufactured all manner of non-essentials; as candies, cakes, and soft drinks; all of which serve not a single useful purpose but *do* feed and incite the passions; acting as a direct incentive to freely indulge in physical gratifications which are responsible for the procreation of countless unwanted children.

Aside from the minority of children and youths employed in the factories and manufacturing establishments where labor is wasted, or worse than wasted, in the production of non-essential and disease-inducing foods and drinks, the majority are slaves to the creation of satins and silks, and the hundred and other things which, though they help to make life more pleasurable for a minority of our citizens, are not essential to either their happiness or welfare.

If the many millions of youths—boys and girls ranging between the age of thirteen to twenty—were to devote their time, say eight hours out of every twenty-four, to the cultivation of food-stuffs, *we could feed the entire world and have a sufficiency left for ourselves. Au contrari,* is it not true that in reducing the number of children born, and with the present tendency of mankind to huddle in cities as do the foxes in holes, there would be fewer to produce the food supply for the many in the cities employed in the manufacture of non-essentials?

Is it not illogical to claim Birth Control necessary merely because millions of children are slaves to factory life, *that their parents may live in squalor in the densely populated cities?* Would it not be far more natural, reasonable, and logical to face the issue squarely and urge that these families now living in poverty move to the country districts and become producers of necessities? One family of five could not only produce all the food required by them, but almost sufficient to support five others, thus relieving the necessity of supplying two families of five who are at present, practically non-producers.

What is the actual reason that the children in foreign countries are starving at the present moment? Is it because these countries are over-populated and unable to produce sufficient food-stuffs, or due to man's inhumanity, necessitating the "murdering off" of the elders to satisfy the depraved mentality of a beast whose mother was, essentially, though possibly unconsciously, a believer in limited progeny, but ignorant of the method to successfully prevent conception; and whose physician evidently was unversed in the modern practice of reducing "something to nothing."

Previous to the time of the world war most countries in Europe were able to supply the greater portion of their food-stuffs. True, in some food an insufficiency existed; but in other commodities there was an abundance, enabling them to exchange and thus to feed their people.

Long before the war the people of France and several other countries commenced to practice Birth Control; in fact, their women had become expert along this line of marital prostitution. Ultimately, what was the result? America was forced to go to the rescue of a glorious country apparently doomed by the invasion of the hordes from a nation breeding like rabbits. Here we have two extremes exemplified. A nation wise to the weaknesses of others, will avoid both.

Admittedly, it is true that we have felt the "nip of deprivation" because of high prices, but let us be honest, was this necessary on acount of insufficient production? Was it due to overpopulation? *Not at all.* In the first place, if one-fifth of the families who today live in large cities, in squalor and misery, and employed in the manufacture of non-essentials such as cigarettes, cigars, silks and satins, and the many other unnecessary commodities, were to leave their wretchedness and migrate to those country homes now rapidly falling prey to the elements, there would be more than a sufficiency of food for the other four-fifths of families employed in producing non-esentials.

Even with the food-stuffs now raised throughout the United States, there would be an ample supply for all, at moderate prices, if this great country had just and enforceable laws, making it *punishable by death* for anyone to buy carloads of potatoes, fruits, vegetables and other edibles, then dumping them into the seas, lakes, and rivers if unsaleable at prices demanded. *This is the actual reason for past high prices, and not the birth of too great a number of children.*

America today has enough uncultivated land to permit every family now living in cities to secure sufficient ground for the production of all the food required for itself and one to three families in foreign countries. Moreover, the one reason European countries lack in food is *because the husbandmen were destroyed in the great war; not from overpopulation.* If the countries in Europe were enabled to feed their people before the war when there were possibly twenty-five million more of them, they can certainly do so now if given an opportunity to use the brain and brawn of their people in cultivation of the soil rather than in rioting, loitering, and manufacturing non-essentials.

An appeal to fanaticism may be condoned in a worthy cause; one with righteousness on its side; but when selfishness, based on sophistry, is its only reason, it cannot be too strongly condemned. Mrs. Sanger continues:

"What shall we women, as citizens of the nation, and of the world, do in this crisis? Shall we continue to bring children into a world that does not, seemingly cannot provide food for them? Shall we continue to build up populations to die in war, or plague, and hunger?"

This plea is irrational, unreasonable, and illogical, and lacking in being unspecific. Who is to feed the children of those of her class who toil not, neither do they spin? Does she imagine it right or just that others, living in the country far from the pleasures and gaieties of the city, shall bring her and her children the product of their toil, while she is free to promulgate a doctrine for the discontinuation of the birth of children? If the few poor hardworking dupes now living in the country did not propagate children as they produce essentials, who would supply the food for even the adults in these thickly settled districts, not considering the children? Does the farmer and his wife wear silks and satins while feeding the chickens, milking the cows and plowing the fields? If not, who does? Is it not those who refuse to help in the raising of crops? Most assuredly! If the class who refuse to help in the cultivation of the soil, and who do not, cannot, appreciate the labor required in the production of food-stuffs expect the workers to bring the food to them, and at prices requiring sacrifices to the farmer and his family, then it would be far better for such to cease the propagation of the specie and live in luxurious marital prostitution until body and soul be burned up by the unholy passion.

The world *can* supply all the food required by her citizens and a great deal more, but it will be necessary that the responsibility for its production be assumed by everyone; instead of these deluding themselves with the idea that a few honest souls should devote eighteen hours of each day to the hardest kind of toil, while enjoying few pleasures, possessing no luxuries; yet supplying the drones with the necessities at starvation prices.

Relative to the question of war, it is certain that a nation which restricts its population is raped by war lords while one with an over-population is not. Germany and France offer an instance which is uncontradictable. For a hundred years prior to the world war the partially insane-degenerate royal families of Germany and her allies encouraged the increase in population,

In France it was different. While it cannot be stated that the government encouraged race suicide, foreign propaganda and its influence on the people of bonny France did so most successfully. What was the result? Germany and her hordes did not greatly respect her for the effort but would quickly have reduced that country to a servility previously unknown among the white peoples had it not been for the heroic efforts of the allies of France. As an absolutely logical fact, the white nation that falls prey to the Birth Control fallacy, irrespective of the *method of procedure,* will sooner or later become the victim of external enemies.

Plagues can hardly be claimed as directly due to an abnormally high birth rate, but to the unnatural congestion of many people in small areas, as in large cities, and the consequent unsanitary conditions resultant on the ignorance and irresponsibility of those flocking together. A country of a million square miles with a like number of inhabitants, might suffer a devastating invasion of the plague if these millions all flocked to one center of habitation, instead of dividing into small units, and establishing themselves on farms and in villages.

Plagues in India are not actually due to the density of the population but to the inertia of the people; this being directly traceable to her negative religion. India also frequently has to contend with hunger, likewise principally the fault of an age-long attempt on the part of many of her citizens to labor as little as possible; her religion ostensibly inculcating the doctrine that one who possesses little is doubly blessed.

China with her fearful scourges of plagues and hunger might reasonably and logically be cited as an example for the active propaganda of Birth Control doctrines; but the teeming denizens of that country will *not* accept the "white man's suicide of Soul" and herein is the danger of teaching it to the pure white race. Mrs. Sanger continues:

"The Governments have been short-sighted in dealing with this problem, and their measures have been pitifully inadequate. They have failed. It is time for the women of the world—for each individual woman to accept her share of the problem. In this hour of crisis and peril, women alone can save the world. They can save it by refusing for five years to bring a child into being. And there is no other way."

What is the government to do? If the millions of her citizens, instead of taking up their habitation on the fertile soil and thus becoming producers, prefer to swarm to the crowded cities as do doves into a raging fire, can the governmental agency legislate against them exercising their right of choice? If these millions become consumers instead of producers, can the government prevent the high prices when due to a demand greater than the supply? If the farmer is forced to sell his chickens because of lack of help, and eggs soar in price can the government prohibit him from selling his stock, or force some denizens of the city to help him care for his flock? If the farmer, for the same reason, must dispose of his valuable milch cows for beef, and the precious babies of the non-producers lack the milk they actually require, can the government squeeze milk out of candies and sodas, silks and satins, cabarets and depraving dance halls? Suppose, for a moment, the women of America would accept Mrs. Sanger at her word and refuse to become mothers, what would be the result? A short time hence the farms would be left without help and then we would see the starvation of those previously born. It is *not* the cities who supply help on the farm —the places for the production of food—but the farms themselves. Possibly the advocates of Birth Control desire only the non-producers of essentials to cease the propagation of the specie, while the century over-worked farmer and his wife are to continue in the same old way. If the apostles of non-production who are attempting to live on the two planes of non-creation— children and essentials—were to devote part of their time inducing the poor of the cities to take up their residence on farms and become producers, thereby also developing respect and potent health and energy, they would have little time to waste accusing the government of faults which are non-existent, nor would they inculcate practices for the prevention of conception which are rapidly destroying the bodies and souls of all who attempt to defy Nature and her laws.

In the same issue of the magazine, under the caption of "Child Labor," we read:

"The truth is that child labor can never be wiped out by legislation. The roots of this evil weed strike deeper than statutes. They spring from the disregard of natural and spiritual laws—they draw their sustenance from overpopulation.

"Where there is but little overpopulation in a class, a region, or a country, there is but little child labor. If there were no over-population at all, there would be no children to toil. While there is a surplus population, under the present social and industrial order, there will be child labor. The result of the efforts of the Child Labor Committee are ample and bitter proof of this sorry truth. Over-populated homes and over-populated communities always produce child labor in some form or other.''

Superficial reasoning! With the exception of a few southern states the youths are employed in the factories and cities in the production of non-essentials. Travel the width and breadth of this great country and comparatively few instances of child slavery will be found existing on the farms, the places of *real* production. Why is this? Because the selfishness and calousness of the people generally in demanding a constantly increasing supply of non-essentials requires not only the services of the vast army of men and women, but also of the children, that their wants may be supplied. Legislation is not required so much for the privilege of teaching Birth Control and marital prostitution as to in some manner reduce the ever-increasing demand for the non-essentials.

If the tax on the actual luxuries were great enough to make these practically prohibitive, the need for workers—slaves to depraved desires—would become less; men would then be employed in the manufacture of these items, thus relieving the children.

Irrespective of all the claims of the Birth Control advocates, the Governmental agencies *could,* and some day will, control child slavery by the enactment and enforcement of rigid laws and the severe punishment of those who exploit the innocent. If, as some seem to think, mankind is become so degraded that no one can be found to right the wrongs of the innocent, then the race is surely doomed, irrespective of anything Race Control apostles may teach.

As long as the universal tendency continues toward the cities, and the desires for the luxuries of life control the actions of the people, to the neglect of the production of the necessities as produced on the farms, there will exist the exploitation of women and children, because the demand for the non-essentials is so great as to require the labor of not only the men who should be devoting their time and energy to other pursuits, but also of countless children as well. Who is to blame? Is it the manufacturer who attempts to supply the demand, or the constantly increasing army of American workers who insist on being supplied with these luxuries? As a matter of fact and common knowledge, is it not now an exploitation of the industrial workers by the industrial workers? Is it not uncontradictable that it is no longer the business men throughout broad America who wear silk shirts, silk hose, silk underwear, and waste their time in cabarets, shows of questionable character, and amusements of doubtful value, but instead, *the millions and millions of workers who constantly demand ever-increasing wages, wherewith to meet the expenses of these luxuries, and at the sacrifice of countless women and children.* Reduce this illegitimate waste, all taking place in the thickly populated centers of habitation, and child labor will, except possibly in a few instances, take care of itself.

If children and women were being exploited in the farming districts, and the fruits of their toil required to warm, clothe, and feed the multitudes, then we would have a problem that only the Infinite could solve; but this is not so, therefore reason can find the solution, if honest men will apply it.

That surplus population is the cause for child labor is illogical. It is a fact that men are given the first opportunity when work is to be done. Naturally, if men have reached a degree of negativeness, such for instance as is universal in India, and refuse to work, then women and children must take their place. If the demand for non-essentials were decreased to a considerable extent, then the number of workers required would likewise be greatly reduced; women and children would be the first dispensed with, and the surplus men would be forced to turn to useful labor and to agricultural pursuits. As the call for luxuries and non-essentials increase so will the exploitation of women and children. Control the first and the second will find its own solution.

Under the title of "Why Bear Children for This?" we read:

"Tuberculosis causes nearly 27 per cent of the deaths of girls who work in any industry between the age of 10 and 14. It claims some of those who escape during the first period after they pass into the fifteen-nineteen period, for then 33 per cent of all the deaths of girls in industry are credited to tuberculosis. In the period from twenty to twenty-four, many of those who have gotten through the first two periods pay the penalty of their enforced servitude during tenderer years, for then the death rate from tuberculosis is 39.8 per cent of the total number of deaths. Nearly 40 per cent—two of every five deaths! This table tells all too well what becomes of factory children."

This article confirms all that we have thus far claimed. It is in the factories, where, with possibly a few exceptions, luxuries are produced; articles in no way prolonging the life of those buying them; serving no useful purpose, and therefore just that much waste in money and energy.

The statements made are undoubtedly true but the conclusions are as misleading as any could possibly be, because they indicate to the average reader that the work in the factory is responsible for this fearful waste of life. *This is absolutely not near the truth.* All things being equal, if the parents of these girls themselves consumed the proper food, such as build strength and create energy; instead of the white breads, starches, sugars and meats to the almost complete exclusion of vital foods, fruits and vegetables; and if these girls were supplied with correct combinations, the factory life would not produce disease or cause the death of one out of ten who now die years before their natural term of life. It is the conglomeration of disease engendering foods; such as pies and sweet cakes, coffee, ice cream and sodas; which the average shop girl consumes, that vitiates their bodies and induces diseases, ultimately ending in death. We know whereof we speak, we have investigated the subject thoroughly during a period of twenty years as Dietitians. We do not wish to be understood as endorsing the factory life for our girls, *we emphatically declare that neither shop nor factory is the place for a girl;* but it is the truth we seek.

Furthermore, the statements made would induce the general public to believe these girls were forced to enter the factory; the word *enforced* being used in the article. It is undoubtedly true that many girls are compelled to work, thus helping in defraying the family expenses, but it is also an uncontradictable fact that a *greater* number of them enter factories of their own free will; even demand the privilege of doing so; homelife being too ordinary and unexciting for them; and these use the greater part of their own earnings for the purchase of fineries in dress and delicacies in food, the proper clothing seemingly too ordinary, while the food that would supply their undernourished bodies with the greatly needed vital forces essential in making health and strength certain, no longer being to their taste.

This globe whereon we live certainly has come to a sorry state if we must cease the procreation of the specie thereby preventing further exploitation of the innocent. Admittedly, if there are no children to enslave, shortly there will be no elders to do so; this would appear to us like "cutting off one's nose to spite the face," hardly a sane procedure. Sensible men and women look to the enactment of just laws; then the strict enforcement of them, even though it should become necessary to court martial a few bribe-takers; backing them against a stone wall as occurs with the enemies of any people; after which the officials selected for the enforcement of law would no doubt be convinced they could no longer deceive the people, nor tamper with their rights and privileges.

In "The Greater Crime," appearing in the same issue, we are further enlightened:

"When I left college I went on a big city newspaper. Here —a "story" a day—were more and ever more examples of the need of Birth Control. A young couple are married; their first child shows the hitherto unthought of syphilistic taint. The frenzied mother kills herself and the child; the man is left to a lifetime of agonized remorse. Of course, they should not have been married; but still less should they have had children."

Propaganda of this nature may possess the possibilities of making converts, but it is neither sane nor logical. In the first place, how was this young man to know he had syphilis? Taking it for granted there was no family history of such inoculation and no reason on his part to suspect it, he naturally would not think of taking the Wasserman test; and even had he done so, there is the possibility of a negative showing; especially when the disease is inherited. What then was he to do? What is any young man to do who has no reason to suspect syphilis? Suppose the child did show the syphilistic taint, it was pitiful, but certainly melodramatic for the mother to kill the child and herself; the disease being curable. We constantly listen to the frigid telling us "thus and so" should not have married; *what* are they to do, being possessed of an abundance of life and energy? Are they to daily be guilty of self-pollution? Do human icebergs think that others, of vastly different nature, can exist as do they? Suppose they are married, how are children to be prevented from coming? Are they to be continually guilty of mutual self-pollution; of the crimes which stamp man as lower than the animals in the field; unfit to face their Maker here and hereafter.

Consider the following by the same author:

"I used to say that if I were ever tempted to marry, I should call on Lottie, and that would cure it! Fortunately for my happiness, she was three thousand miles away when that temptation did assail me, and so I yielded. But there is no danger of my falling into the slough of despond which is drowning her—I married a man of the twentieth, not the eighteenth century. Whether or not we shall ever have a child depends on circumstances beyond the control of either of us. But until then I am free to do my own work, made more worth while through the joys of love and companionship, without the haunting fear of unwanted maternity—of thrusting the burden of life on another human being, without being able to guarantee it at least a fair chance in a decent world."

What are we coming to in this so-called enlightened age? It is an absolute law in the Spiritual, as well as in the natural world, that marriage brings with it the responsibilities of parentage. To be sure, they did set aside this divine fiat in old Greece, but consider what happened.

There can be no love without passion; and it is self-evident that when the average wedded pair exercise the creative function and results do not become apparent, there must be abuse somewhere in the relationship. There are many contraceptions, but none of them are absolutely certain; and as previously stated, most of them are detrimental to the well-being of those participating. If the instructions we have perused and proported as coming from the Birth Control advocates are authentic, then it would be far better for the average man and woman to continue in their former manner of life and have children than to damn themselves body and soul.

Whosoever marries and shuns the responsibilities of parentage must commit conjugal fraud in one form or another as is apparent from the universal testimony of all who have confessed to us their experience; and though we are willing to believe this lady married a man of the twentieth century, we would remind ourselves that even Greece, centuries ago, had men, *also taught by women,* who were wise in the ways of cultured prostitution, and these, like their female instructors, all faithful devotees to the Birth Control cultus, now "lie amoulding in their graves," while even Sappho's wonderful poems are unknown except in legend.

In an interview with a "World" correspondent, and appearing in the issue of December 26, Mrs. Sanger, anent her desire for a law in New York legalizing birth control clinics, is purported to have said:

"If we had a law that permitted the establishment of birth control clinics I believe that within one generation we would wipe out a large proportion of the insanity in the United States, and cure 90 per cent. of our social evils."

We flatly contradict this statement. The knowledge of "preventive conception" by one means or another, is becoming almost universal. Various methods are resorted to, all more or less successful. Speaking from experience gained from listening to many confessions, generally those who practice the various "arts" indulge more freely than when men and women embrace in God's old fashioned way, due to the expectation that they will be able to escape the consequences of their act. Result: Seeking the pleasure of frequent indulgence, but hoping to avoid the penalty, my lady accidently doth conceive; her mind is constantly on the thought of not wanting the child; impressing this on the child's mentality, preventing a normal development of the mental faculties, as also interfering with natural bodily growth; and a mentally defective, physically perverted, or moral leper is born. In the aggregate this is a daily occurrence, and as a consequence, the total of undesirables in the proportion of births, is greater than ever before.

Any prevention of conception not based on the sterile period between the lunar seasons of the woman, or on the failure of the uterus to "draw in" the seminal fluid because of the side embrace, is a perversion, and—the woman always pays.

Mrs. Sanger is reported to have made the assertion she had brought the message from Europe's most distinguished scientists, diplomats and economists, that: "We agree with the advocates of birth control that no world peace is possible without a reduction of the birth rate and immediate action toward its international accomplishment."

Irrespective of who voiced this sentiment, facts flatly contradict; more than this, clearly indicate if this advice be followed, instead of preventing war, it will be the direct incentive for another and greater war wherein the white race will be swept to its doom.

The white race has reached the turning point; it is practically stationary at present, and unless a supreme effort is made, will commence to recede; while the wave of the colored races will sweep onward.

Up to the present moment the white race has had the advantage because of its initiative and inventive power; it has exploited almost every land; its agencies have been established everywhere; its destructive forces found foothold on every soil, thereby reducing both in potency and number the natives of that soil. Where the native population was not dispersed, it was dominated, always to the advantage of the conquerors.

For centuries, by one means or another, but generally through cults having at heart the bestial sexual debasement of mankind, like those rampant in Sodom, Gomorrha, Babylon, Greece, and Rome, the race has periodically been guilty of race suicide; and to this has recently been added, through the war, the appalling loss of possibly 35,000,000 of white men who should have become the fathers of sturdy youngsters. Another war, especially if of the colored races—yellow, red, brown and black, against the white, aided by the destructive machinery and methods now known to the dark races as to the white, and an age old institution will be reversed—the white man will become the slave of the colored.

Formerly there appeared little to fear; the darker races did not possess either the initiative or the aggressiveness of the white; over-population was chronic with some of them; they were held in check by plagues, pestilence, and famine; totally ignorant of the means to combat the reaper; all these keeping them in check. Now it is vastly different; the white race has discovered the means of overcoming disease, and has taught the methods to his colored brothers; awakening in them also the desire for conquest; and now, slowly but surely, they are overcoming *all* the forces which formerly held them in subjection, and the population of many races is increasing so rapidly that emigration is becoming larger and larger; and sooner or later, whether we will or not, the crisis must be faced.

As previously stated, the population of the world is about one-third white, heretofore a race of progression and aggression while the colored races were sleeping the sleep of inertia. *Now they are waking to their possibilities and beginning to work in unison,* while the white race is becoming inoculated with *perversia sexualis;* a desire for all the pleasures of indulgence while seeking to avoid natural results; stooping to every known manner of beastly practices in order to control conception; and to this is added the internal struggle of man against man. Woe to those who will not heed the writing in the sky.

The advocates of Race Control, formerly known as race suicide, inadvertently admit this, as note:

'For unless we apply fundamental remedies to these conditions we will fast approach the same congested and confused state which may and is likely to produce an outburst of the same nature as the European struggle that in four years laid a world in ruin." Note that it was only the countries of the white races. *"We shall come to find ourselves in the same position as Japan, of whom we read even in the most conservative press the ominous portent of her overwhelming and rising tide of population. There are those who even prophesy that a war is looming anew because of Japan's struggle to support this overcrowded condition of society. There will be the same excuses as those of Germany for her aggressive efforts at conquest—a place for her population—but a second disaster will be infinitely more terrible and death-dealing."*

We have italicised the above statements to call especial attention to them, proving, as they do, part of our contention. Can any sane man believe that such an aggressive action on the part of the yellow race can be stopped by retarding the birth of healthy progeny among the white? When we have finally committed race suicide and the hordes are ready to descend upon us, committing on our children and women the crimes of which the Hun in Europe was guilty, will they stop when the apostles of Birth Control lift their guilty hands and call: "Cease, see ye not we have discontinued the propagation of our kind, therefore you must not attempt to take our lands and rape our women and children, nor make slaves of our effeminate men, who have so nobly obeyed our behests."

In conclusion, we seek to appear on record as favoring Birth Control under certain conditions and circumstances, as:

When either husband or wife, or both, are not possessed of health, therefore liable to give birth to undesirables.

When the father is not in position to reasonably support more than a limited number of children.

We further emphatically declare that we do not condemn a man because he smokes, imbibes what seems pleasing to him, or wears silken socks or shirts; nor would we look askance at a woman if she likes her candies and creams, and prefers the fineries to the commonplace and essential; nor do we advocate the restriction of the colored races; we merely face facts squarely and without reservation; placing the blame for present conditions where it rightly belongs; at the same time pointing to the danger line ahead, beyond which flow rivers of human blood.

CPSIA information can be obtained
at www.ICGtesting.com
Printed in the USA
BVHW060228130421
604735BV00011B/1005